Fro...
Natura...
Therapies

JUDY JACKA has been involved with medical work and health since the age of sixteen. Preparation for her professional career included laboratory work at two leading Melbourne hospitals, general nursing training at Melbourne's Prince Henry hospital, naturopathic training at the Southern School of Natural Therapies, and a post-graduate diploma in Human Relations Education at Melbourne College of Advanced Education. She has in addition been working with the Arcane School for fifteen years, and this has enabled her to make a bridge between the Eastern and Western approaches to health and disease. She was Principal of the Southern School of Natural Therapies from 1971 to 1988 and is at present chairperson of the college board.

Frontiers of Natural Therapies

Judy Jacka N.D., Grad. Dep. H.R.E.

LOTHIAN PUBLISHING COMPANY PTY LTD
MELBOURNE   SYDNEY   AUCKLAND

To those who enjoy the adventure and responsibility
involved in the search for true health and well-being

A Lothian Book
Lothian Publishing Company Pty Ltd
11 Munro Street, Port Melbourne, Victoria 3207

First published 1989
Copyright © Judy Jacka 1989

National Library of Australia
Cataloguing-in-Publication data

Jacka, Judy, 1938– .
    Frontiers of Natural Therapies

    Includes index.
    ISBN 0 85091 348 9.

    1. Alternative medicine. I. Title.

615.5

Edited by Lee White
Typeset by Solo Typesetting, South Australia
Printed by The Book Printer, Maryborough

Foreword

Now is the time for a comprehensive book to be published outlining the basis and practice of natural therapies. Interest and controversy about natural therapies has increased in recent years. Natural therapies have undergone two public inquiries in Victoria since 1973 and public patronage has increased to the point where almost one Victorian in ten consulted an 'alternative' therapist in 1985.

Far from providing a standard outline of the accepted natural therapies, Judy Jacka entertains and enlightens by taking us to the leading edge of naturopathic practice in the world today. Not only are we given clear frameworks to help us understand herbal, vitamin and mineral therapy, homoeopathy and iridology, for example, but Judy Jacka also introduces us to areas often considered too difficult for rigorous explanation. For instance, she explores energy fields, Vega-testing, psychosomatics and meditation, Eastern healing and the Chakras, and spiritual healing. Even more impressive is how she integrates for the reader these many and varied aspects of the philosophy and practice of natural therapies.

Readers with scientific training may find inadequate data has been provided fully to consider some of the theories outlined. However, all people with open minds will be stimulated by considering some of the ideas that are proposed. Over the centuries intuitive sensings and unexplained observations have opened up many areas of knowledge for human beings. On the other hand, Judy Jacka questions the scientifically based suppression of bodily symptoms in much of modern medical practice. She argues: why suppress problems and therefore make them worse when the underlying physical and psychological causes can be attended to? This issue certainly lends itself to further (healthy) debate in interdisciplinary circles in the future.

At the end of this book Judy Jacka excites us with her vision of the future of medicine, of health care in Australia. First, she presents a strong case for the registration of natural therapists to ensure a high standard of care can be provided for the growing number of natural therapy patients. She also argues that integration and co-operation between complementary (not alternative) medicine and orthodox medicine is not just a matter of common sense but a necessary, if not inevitable, step for the Australian community to take.

In the midst of all the current debate about the place of different health techniques and modalities, Judy Jacka refers to the soul as the source of all healing. Maybe as doctors and therapists alike align themselves with this healing source, healing may come to the health field as well as individual patients!

Welcome to this eminently readable and timely book.

Richard Hetzel, MB, BS

Contents

Introduction

The general aim of this book is to explore the practice and principles of natural therapies and, wherever possible, to provide a scientific framework for the concepts which are discussed. I have paid particular attention to exploring the two main tenets of naturopathic philosophy—the vitalistic model for disease, that is, improving vitality and balancing energies, and the problem of internal toxaemia or toxic waste elimination—both from the point of view of the medical and physical sciences and through naturopathic clinical findings and practice.

As in my other books, I have explored the relationship between the subtle energies, the inner constitution and health or disease, including extra information on the application of these principles to health on a wider scale, in terms of humanity and the planet as a whole. This information is based on trans-Himalayan teachings, plus my own studies, meditation, and reflection over a period of twenty-five years. There is increasing public interest in this more esoteric area, due in part to the practical experience of improved health through meditation practices, so any dissertation on health and disease is benefited by inclusion of these more subjective factors.

I have devoted a chapter to making a synthesis of the various main therapies including vitamins, minerals, herbs, homoeopathy and flower essences. For a detailed application of these therapies to the wide range of disorders treated by natural therapists, I refer the reader to my book, *A-Z of Natural Therapies*.

I have also included an introduction to the growing practice of functional diagnosis using electronic instruments such as Vegatesting. This area of medicine is now widely accepted in Europe amongst both doctors and natural therapists and is expected to expand quickly in Australia over the next few years.

Some of the medical scientific work that is discussed is new and for this reason not widely published in scientific literature. As so often happens with pioneering work which at first seems out on a limb, in a few years we may look back to see the challenging work of Becker and Reid, for example, as a leading edge of medical science in the 1980s.

Controversial as some of the models for health and disease may seem, it should be stressed that natural therapies are really based on common sense. It is common sense to natural therapists that a good life-style and the use of particular natural medicines will improve immunity so that there is a lower incidence of infections and chronic disease. It is also basic good sense that everyone should be treated holistically and as a unique individual with his or her particular needs.

By developing natural medicine on common sense, certain therapy models have evolved which people choose because they get results to their problems. This book is devoted to exploring the various models for acute and chronic disease. It considers diagnostic models which indicate the immense difference between one person and another, and looks at models for treatment which have persisted through public demand and not because of any official sanction or support. I have also considered some sociological factors including the new model which is developing as a bridge between orthodox medicine and the complementary approaches which form the main subject matter of this book.

There is in addition, a chapter on a totally new approach to psychology using natural therapies, meditation and the teaching of the subjective factors to clients. The clients involved in this new development are having holistic therapy in the broadest and deepest sense, and have the satisfaction not only of resolving their own problems but of helping the others in the group.

There are case histories throughout the book to bring the various concepts alive: it is not possible to include a large number of them, but there is enough information to help the reader understand the application of the principles discussed.

It is my hope that this book will give greater understanding of the principles and practice of natural therapies whether the reader is a student, client or practitioner. The sphere of natural therapies is exciting and creative because it works with the life energies which shape our universe. Practical ways have been found to use these energies in the form of natural medicine to restore life and meaning to an increasing number of individuals.

CHAPTER 1

The Main Therapies and Their Blending

How can we know which of the many therapies is suitable for a particular condition? Why are there so many natural therapies? Are there a few well established therapies which will cover all ailments? Can several different therapies be used at the same time?

The following therapies are now readily available in many large cities throughout the Western world: acupressure, acupuncture, Alexander technique, aromatherapy, chiropractic, colour healing, electro-acupuncture, foot reflexology, herbal medicine, homoeopathy, kinesiology, massage, magnetic healing, meditation, mineral therapy, osteopathy, psychic healing, Reiki, spiritual healing, Tai Chi, Touch For Health, vitamin therapy and Vivaxis, as well as a number of sub-divisions and lesser known therapies.

The best way to approach the subject is first to examine what it is in general that most natural therapies achieve. All natural therapies promote the two main criteria for health: improving vitality and balancing energies plus assisting the elimination of toxic waste from the body via the usual channels. The balancing of energies usually features work with the chakras or meridian systems (see Chapter 10) and is found in acupuncture, acupressure, Reiki, magnetic healing, meditation, reflexology, psychic healing, spiritual healing, Tai Chi, Touch

For Health, aromatherapy and colour healing. Herbal medicine, vitamin and mineral therapy and homoeopathy are therapies which influence the biochemistry, improving lymphatic drainage and promoting excretion of toxic waste as a result of such balancing of the biochemistry.

There is an overlapping between these two groups for once the energies are improved elimination is automatically increased. Conversely, once toxic waste is removed there is an improvement in energy. In the case of homoeopathy, both functions appear to take place simultaneously and this applies to some extent with all the other therapies. The term holistic may therefore be used in connection with all these areas of therapy. Damage to cells or tissues never results from these approaches and that is why these therapies are classed as natural. This does not mean that there is no associated discomfort. In the case of established cases of arthritis or severe skin disorders there may be considerable temporary discomfort as the body clears itself of waste.

The veritable explosion of natural medicine and healing is continuing with new approaches and knows no bounds. The average person is concerned to know whether a particular therapy has been established long enough to be considered safe and useful. I will therefore chiefly describe the basis for the most traditional and widespread therapies and will indicate how these have been married together to provide for a synthesis in treating a variety of ailments. For a description of this process as applied to the full range of disorders, the reader is referred to my previous book.[1]

The most widely known and oldest therapy throughout the world is herbal medicine. Records of physicians using herbs for healing is contained in every culture: in Africa, the Middle East, India, North America, South America, China, Australia and Europe (the home of modern herbal medicine). It is generally accepted that the herbs growing naturally in a particular place are the ones most likely to be needed for people living in that area. For instance, the plant Arnica Montana grows in the mountains where it is used for falls,

A Synthesis of Therapies

MINERALS
The Basic Building Blocks

VITAMINS
Promote Vital Energies

HERBS
Improve Organ Function

HOMOEOPATHY
Removes Inherited Taints

BACH FLOWERS
Restores Emotional Balance

ACUPUNCTURE
Balances Body Energy

MANIPULATION
Restores Structural Balance

MEDITATION
Integrates All Levels of Being

sprains and bruises. The blood cleansing plant, Bugle, is growing thickly along the edges of our house and nowhere else on
our 1·2 ha property. Is it a coincidence that at that place, toxic
chemicals may be present as a result of the compulsory spraying
below the concrete slab ordered by the local council?

Overview of Herbal Medicine

An anthropologist by the name of Solecki has produced evidence
that botanic medicine was practised 60000 years ago in Iraq.
The floor of a grave was found to be rich in flower pollen
grains which must have been carefully gathered.[2] Seven out of
eight of these species are currently used by naturopaths and
orthodox doctors in clinical practice. In ancient times within
hunter gatherer societies, the use of herbal remedies required
some knowledge of botany, skill in preparation, plus clinical
observation of the effect from the plant on patients so that
prescription guidelines could be made. Botanic gardens had
been developed by 1500 BC and there was a profitable herb
trade in the countries around the Mediterranean with Arabia
and Asia Minor.[3] Indian Ayurvedic medicine is 5000 years old
and Chinese herbal medicine is perhaps older.[4] The systems of
health care which have developed from these cultures provide
the basis for many modern investigations into medicinally
active plants and their constituents.

The areas of orthodox medicine, botany and botanic
medicine have only been separate disciplines since the
eighteenth century. There is a considerable overlap still occurring as herbal medicine has gained from scientific research into
plants, while orthodox medicine on the other hand, continues
to use plant extracts in 25 per cent of drugs.[5] The father of
Western medicine, Hippocrates, stressed the need to provide
those forms of treatment which assisted the recuperative powers
of the patient through diet, climate and exercise and he
included use of herbal remedies.[6] He established the practice of
taking a careful case history of the idiosyncrasies of the patient.

Galen was a famous herbal physician of the third century who followed Hippocrates in some respects. The herbal physician Theophrastus of Eresus (372–286 BC) was an early and distinguished botanist who established an extensive botanic garden as a result of receiving field reports and specimens from many Alexandrian doctors. He wrote fifteen volumes from his observations.[7] The herbal *Materia Medica* which was used until the Renaissance was compiled by Dioscorides. In this work, six hundred plants are considered in terms of their appearance, habitat, preparation, action, contra-indications and uses. In the sixteenth century Paracelsus, a Swiss physician, challenged the status quo with his own observations which included the Doctrine of Signatures. Under this system herbs were chosen according to their similarity to the patient's organs and needs. For example, herbs with a deep yellow juice were given for problems with the bile, or leaves in the shape of a lung were give for bronchial problems.

From being a respectable profession with high social status, the practice of herbal medicine gradually developed in different directions. Physicians began to use herbs with less discrimination and to combine harsh purgatives with leechings and the use of heavy metals like mercury and arsenic. The other approach attracted simple people such as peasants, and Benedictine monks who used folk medicines without the intellectual precision of earlier centuries. Their treatments tended to be slow and gentle whereas the orthodox medicine of the time developed the prejudice that treatment must be speedy and spectacular regardless of side-effects. Herbal medicine was seen to be primitive by the orthodox physician who explained to the patients that if a herb contains any value it is best to use the active ingredient in concentrated form.

Herbal medicines may be analysed into a large number of constituents including carbohydrates, minerals and trace elements, vitamins, alkaloids, oils, resins, mucilages, gums, tannins and other properties. The active principles are those constituents which are considered to be the therapeutic agents of the plants. Research has not yet confirmed fully the relationship between the various constituents and the clinical effects. Because living cells respond to minute amounts of organic and inorganic substances, it is suggested that some properties of plants which have not yet been identified may be responsible for pronounced therapeutic effects. For this reason natural therapists prefer to use the whole plant rather than the isolated active constituent. There appears to be a balancing effect in the use of the whole plant which reduces any side-effect to an absolute minimum. Unfortunately, clinical trials using the whole plant are almost non-existent as yet.

Due to the fact that herbal medicine has such a long and recorded history, it could be classed as having the longest clinical trials in the history of medicine. *The British Herbal Pharmacopoeia* is the bible of most modern Western herbalists. It lists 228 therapeutic indications for the herbs which include monographs on most of the botanical agents in use. There is a definition of each herb, microscopic and macroscopic description of the dried form, notes on dosage, contra-indications, and therapeutic uses. Herbs are usually administered orally but may be applied externally in the form of ointments, lotions and liniments. Where water is used as the means of extraction, the medicine is called an infusion or decoction. Tinctures and extracts are more popular as they involve extraction through a mixture of water plus alcohol and are therefore preserved for some time. Capsules of dried preparation and solid extracts are also used and these are a handy form for ingestion by modern patients.

The main value of herbal medicine in clinical practice is to assist elimination of toxins and to tone and regulate organ function. As a result, the homoeostasis or balance of the body is restored. Herbs are unsurpassable in this repect, especially in acute cases. In the case of children and babies they need to be used in diluted or homoeopathic form as sick children will rarely drink a strong herbal mixture. To give mineral, vitamin and constitutional homoeopathic remedies without first using herbs for organ therapy and to assist elimination through bowel, lungs, skin, and kidneys is a limited approach.

It depends on the particular health problem as to which channel for elimination will be encouraged, and this in turn governs the selection of herbs. For instance, in the case of a sluggish bowel, the liver is often found to be congested, and in cases of eczema the lymphatic system, liver and kidneys may need attention. For bronchitic conditions we may select liver, lymphatic and bronchial herbs. The reader will have noted that in a number of the case histories given in this text the liver showed up as a stressed organ. It is almost standard procedure to give a few herbs in extract or homoeopathic form for the liver. It is a very important organ for the purpose of detoxification and, through toning the liver, elimination through all channels is aided. This is because the liver has the basic role to deal with all toxins in the body whether from drugs, chemicals or food.

_____ CASE HISTORY _____

The following case is a typical one where there was a history of severe headaches which basically related to a toxic factor. Angela, aged forty-two, came to the clinic with a history of continual headaches which affected the sides and back of the head. She had several per month and they were worse at menstruation. Her diet was only fair and the regular consumption of ham, coffee and cheese had added to the congestion of the liver which was found by Vegatesting (see Chapter 5) to be the most stressed organ, followed by the large bowel.

The first month of treatment emphasised the liver treatment with a solid extract tablet containing Dandelion, Wahoo, Fringe Tree and Centaury plus Carduus Mar, Chelidonium, Hydrastis, and Dandelion in homoeopathic form. She was also given vitamin C to help the detoxification process and vitamin B-complex, potassium phosphate and magnesium phosphate for general nerve toning. After one month, she reported that headaches occurred less often and were less severe. The liver was no longer showing as a stressed organ by Vega analysis and the 'biological age' had reduced (see Chapters 4 and 5). At the following visit, headaches were still present but not severe. She reported a painful period with clots. With natural treatment it is not uncommon for elimination of waste to take place in women via the menstrual cycle. For the clotting tendency, a specially prepared mineral salt (potassium chloride) was given. At this point in the treatment, homoeopathic drops were added for lymphatic drainage. These were based on the herbs Iris Vericolour, and the mineral Hepar Sulphuricus.

Over the next few months, headaches gradually disappeared altogether and the remedies were tapered off after eight months of treatment. It may be asked if the liver was the main problem, why bother with the rest of the treatment? It is here that the synthesis of remedies can be explained. In the days when herbal medicine first flourished vitamin C was unknown, although we now know from analysis that plants and herbs can be very rich in this vitamin. It has been found in naturopathic practice that we can speed up the treatment process with the addition of vitamin C. This is due to the fact that vitamin C has a strong detoxifying effect of its own. Therefore, as the toxins are released from the connective tissue, provided there is plenty of vitamin C circulating in the system, many of the unpleasant side-effects of the healing process can be avoided. In acute cases of infection, the vitamin C will be increased until what is known as bowel threshold level is reached, that is, until the bowel becomes loose.

In the case of Angela, she was also given vitamin B-complex and a mineral salt for the nervous system. Once again, we need to consider natural medicine in a modern context. Due to modern farming methods, the soils and consequently foods have become depleted in vitamins and minerals. It is found that headaches do not disappear completely with just the detoxification programme. The nervous tension of headaches is often partly due to a deficiency in magnesium phosphate, the main salt needed to prevent nerve and muscle spasm.

Mineral Therapy

Publicity in recent years has increased awareness of common mineral supplements such as calcium, iron and zinc. However, mineral therapy has been used in particular forms by natural therapists for many decades. One of the most popular branches developed in the last century from the pioneering work of a doctor named Schussler. He used twelve mineral salts to remove basic mineral disturbances at the cellular level. In those days actual deficiencies were not a main problem; rather he worked to correct the homoeostatic balance so that the minerals could be more readily assimilated from the diet.[8]

The mineral disturbances were diagnosed by signs and symptoms in the clinical state of the patient. Minerals were prescribed in low-potency homoeopathic doses. Tissue salt therapy as it is called has enjoyed world-wide popularity and has been used successfully by many lay people. It has proved a simple and safe form of medication and has enabled patients to avoid the use of drugs and in some cases surgery. Due to the dietary and farming changes over the last fifty years, nowadays this type of mineral therapy is not so useful in all cases. We tend now to use larger amounts of the same mineral salts but they are still prepared with great emphasis on the mixing process so that they become very assimilable. Blackmore laboratories in Sydney, Australia, are world leaders in this field and have been followed by other manufacturers. The Blackmore range of mineral salts are named Celloids and are the most widely prescribed range of minerals throughout Australia.[9]

The reader would have noticed from the previous case history involving Angela that when using a synthesis of remedies it is rather difficult to isolate any single factor in the treatment programme as the most significant. Nevertheless, in the following case I would say that the antispasmodic action of magnesium could be classed as the most important issue.

————————— CASE HISTORY —————————

Lynette, aged forty-five, had been hospitalised recently for continual severe pain in the left loin. A kidney stone had been removed twenty months previously. Other earlier surgery involved removal of the gall-bladder four years ago, stomach stapling to help obesity, and a hysterectomy five years earlier following ovarian problems. She was currently on ovarian hormone replacement therapy plus thyroxin for an under-active thyroid. The iris revealed an open structure (weak constitution) with weaknesses mainly appearing in the bronchial area and kidneys. Vega analysis was more specific and indicated that the left ureter was the main problem—a plastic lining for this ureter following removal of the kidney stone had previously been rejected. Her diet was fairly good as a result of watching her weight and from restricting heavy protein to prevent further kidney stones.

After the examination, observation and analysis of the case, I decided that the pain was probably resulting from spasm in the ureter and therefore the first two weeks of treatment emphasised the mineral magnesium phosphate. This was combined with the antispasmodic herbs Valerian, Scullcap, and Vervain plus liver and lymphatic herbs in homoeopathic dosage for cleansing. Vitamin B6 and B-complex completed the first prescription and was given to augment the magnesium effect. On her return visit she reported improving in three days and only having a few spasms. The ureter was no longer showing stress via Vega analysis. Magnesium phosphate in the 30th potency was added to consolidate assimilation of magnesium from the diet in the future. The supplements were continued for several more months to resolve the mineral deficiency. There was no severe relapse at the time of writing, although Lynette found that when she reduced the magnesium prematurely, some discomfort returned.

All parts of the prescription had their role to play, but we often find a magnesium deficiency in the case of formation of stones.[10] In this case history the general deficiency had left a tendency to spasm in the body although there was no stone present. The resolving of this deficiency will help prevent future stones. The combination of B6 and magnesium has been found useful in this connection and underscores again the synergistic aspects of prescribing.

Trace Elements

In recent years natural therapists have become conscious of the need to include trace elements in their synthesis of prescribing. As an example, in the case of diabetes, the trace element chromium can be a vital additional factor which is needed to promote maximum use of sugar by the weak pancreas. Its role in the glucose tolerance factor has now been demonstrated and it has been found essential for fat and sugar metabolism.[11] The trace element would be used in conjunction with digestive herbs, tissue salts, and vitamins. Another example of blending would be the use of the trace element zinc in the case of under-sized children who may also have other signs of zinc deficiency. The tissue salt calcium phosphate is often used to promote healthy growth but in the absence of zinc, many metabolic chains in the body are inadequate.[12]

_____CASE HISTORY _____

Tom, aged six, had given his family cause for great concern. He was only able to use his bowels once or twice every two weeks and this with considerable discomfort and trauma due to the enormous size of the stool. His life at school was becoming affected by the situation. He slept and ate well but was very tired and undersized for his age. The lack of growth was typical for a zinc deficiency. As a baby there was a history of regurgitation involving the cardiac sphincter of the stomach.

The iris (see Chapter 2) did not reveal anything of great significance apart from moderate indication for lack of bowel tone. The bowel was indicated as the most stressed organ via Vega analysis. The first month of treatment included zinc and calcium phosphate for his lack of growth, potassium phosphate for improving nerve tone to the bowel, calcium fluoride in homoeopathic dosage for restoring elasticity to the bowel, and liver and lymphatic homoeopathic remedies for detoxification. A homoeopathic antidote to particular toxins was also administered.

On his return visit, the bowel was found to have been much more regular but the stools were still very large. This is not surprising as the bowel would have become very lacking in tone. The remedies were continued and after two months the bowel was working every two days. The 'biological age' of the bowel had returned to normal. After four months of the continued treatment improvement was maintained and there had been a spurt of growth of several inches in height. As with most cases, a synthesis of remedies was needed. The zinc deficiency was very prominent and as a trace element with many biochemical purposes in relation to other minerals and vitamins, its deficiency formed a basic part of the clinical picture.

Selenium is another trace element often needed in the supportive role of an anti-oxidant for it can help preserve the integrity of cell membranes. This is presumably why it has been found to be protective against cancer of breast, colon, and liver. This trace element is commonly found to be depleted in soils where the cancer incidence is higher than the national average. In guarding against cancer, this mineral is often combined with vitamins A, C and E which also have anti-oxidant properties. The synergistic effect of minerals and vitamins continues to be noted. The minerals are also inter-dependent and this underscores that supplements should not be given indiscriminately or in isolation to any great extent. For instance, zinc displaces copper and if consumed in large quantities over a long period can lead to anaemia from a copper deficiency. Calcium and magnesium are also mutually antagonistic and as some of the deficiency signs are common to both minerals, training and discrimination is needed on the part of the therapist.

Vitamin Therapy

As this chapter is designed to describe how the various main established therapies work together, the individual vitamins and their uses will not be described. There are many excellent publications which deal with this area.[13] In reality, vitamins are catalysts for various foodchains and metabolic pathways. Their isolation and identification from particular plants, grains and fruits is comparatively recent and most interest in this subject has taken place in the last fifty years. As part of clinical nutrition, vitamin therapy must be considered to be very well established in Western society.

Those opposed to vitamin therapy argue that we gain our Recommended Daily Allowance (RDA's) from a well-balanced diet. They do not explain how one can have a well-balanced diet in the presence of pollution, depleted soils, insecticides and the stress of twentieth-century living. There is no doubt that people buy vitamins indiscriminately, wasting money and time. When carefully selected, especially when combined with mineral therapy on a fairly short term basis, vitamins can give spectacular results. Examples would be in the area of acute infection with bacteria or virus, acute phases of eczema and dermatitis, and acute nervous disorders like Bell's palsy and shingles.[14]

A recommended daily allowance is meaningless due to individual needs and environmental differences. During an infection for instance, the body uses up large quantities of vitamin C. This can be proved in a simple way by noting the difference in the amounts of the vitamin which cause diarrhoea in the same person when healthy and when suffering from an infection. This is called bowel threshold level for vitamin C. The same logic could be applied to urinary excretion of vitamin B-complex for instance before and during Bell's palsy. The changing need for vitamin C could be fairly easily established through simple biochemical tests.

Vitamin and Mineral Therapy Combined

Many of our clients now visit the clinic having first spent considerable sums of money at the local health food store on vitamins or multi vitamin/mineral tablets. Some of the products in this range are carefully designed and provide a good general tonic for the person who has insufficient time or interest to give themselves a good diet. Others contain so little of each constituent that unless the person has an appalling diet, little is gained from including the supplement. In either case, the average person needs some organ toning and detoxification and in the face of years of accumulated waste, the supplement would not be adequately absorbed. The pure herbalist may argue that herbs contain sufficient vitamins and that they are rich in mineral salts. Until this century, this statement would have been correct. We live in times of unprecedented stress both in terms of pollution and speed of life-style. Combining these factors with the deficient farming methods has provided the need for much larger amounts of vitamins and minerals than are found to occur in herbs.

This does not mean that a person needs to be on vitamin and mineral supplements for long periods of time. The cells require a number of substances to maintain and promote the homoeo-static or balancing factors crucial to health. These substances include not only fats, carbohydrates, proteins and water but also minerals, trace elements, vitamins, co-enzymes and other metabolites. Once the biochemical balance has been restored through supplementation, and this averages about six months, the balance can usually be obtained through a good diet and life-style.

When the naturopathic movement began in Germany during the middle of the last century, food was largely unrefined and unpolluted. Flour was not refined to remove husk and germ, nor were flavourings, colourings or preservatives, bleaches, emulsifiers and other chemicals added to foodstuffs. At the time, natural therapists found it sufficient to educate people to consume a diet balanced adequately between cereals, vegetables, fruits and animal products. Research on cereals, grains and vegetables produced by modern farming methods shows a depletion of mineral content when compared to levels found in food before the Second World War.[15] Until the 1940s, farmers still used crop rotation and allowed the land to lie fallow between the crops so that the soil could be replenished by slow but time-tested methods. The use of superphosphate has sped crop production but has taken its toll through reduction of humus in the pasture and consequent mineral imbalance.

The influence of heredity will be discussed in Chapter 11 and the tubercular miasm is described there. In this particular problem it is found that the body is unable to utilise calcium. Children with a tendency towards asthma and bronchial problems are found to need calcium in very assimilable forms to resolve the deficiency. In keeping with the theme of synthesis in practice, the giving of the homoeopathic nosodes at the same time as the detoxifying herbs and mineral supplementation enables the child to absorb the calcium more adequately from the diet. The synthesis needed in prescribing is therefore obvious as the three approaches of vitamin/mineral supplementation, herbal detoxification and homoeopathic miasmatic and constitutional prescribing is needed for the average asthma case.

_____ CASE HISTORY _____

Joanna, aged ten, is a good case to illustrate the synthesis in prescribing for asthma. She had suffered from bronchial asthma for three years and had been given copious antibiotics with little result. The iris revealed lymphatic congestion and the lymphatic glands were indicated by Vega analysis as the main cause of the problem. Her condition was worse with changes in weather indicating the hydrogonoid constitution which gives asthma associated with a particular inherited constitution. This inherited factor will be explained in Chapter 11. A few years earlier Joanne had only suffered recurrent colds and the involvement of the chest indicated that the inherited disposition was starting to take hold more deeply in the constitution.

During the first month, most of the treatment was directed towards eliminating toxins and stimulating the lymphatic and immune system. To this end, the mineral combination of iron phosphate and potassium chloride, vitamin C, liver and lymphatic herbs in homoeopathic form were all included. An antispasmodic herbal tincture which includes Thyme and Ammi Visnagi was given for the actual asthma attacks. After one month it was reported that Joanne had a cough for one week but no asthma. The 'biological age' for the lymphatic system had improved considerably. The treatment was continued with the addition of a herbal cough tablet to be used if necessary. Apart from a severe bout of sneezing during the next month there were no problems.

The problem had now moved outwards from the chest to the sinus which is a good sign as natural healing moves from deep within the body outwards. The remedies were repeated for another month and there was no asthma and only a bit of sneezing. At this stage the homoeopathic miasmatic remedy (see Chapter 11) was given in the form of Thuja in the 200th potency and a weekly dose was prescribed for two months. This cleared up the sinus problem.

Joanne was monitored at sparse intervals throughout the winter but there was no relapse with asthma; any colds were minor and easily handled with a few remedies. Her mother has sent numerous asthmatic children to our clinic as a result of Joanne's improvement.

There is a synergy between the vitamins and minerals themselves apart from the blending of the three main therapies mentioned in the previous case. This is a most interesting facet of naturopathic prescribing. For instance, when treating colds, flu and all infections, we use a mineral tablet containing iron phosphate and potassium chloride in a specially prepared form using a mixing process not unlike the preparation of homoeopathic remedies. The iron component of this tablet which is used for its anti-inflammatory effect is more easily absorbed into the cell in the presence of vitamin C. Depending on the type of infection, other mineral salts may be needed—potassium sulphate is used for greenish discharges and calcium sulphate for discharges which tend to be continuous.

Another example of synergy is that between the vitamin B-complex group and magnesium and potassium phosphate which we use so often for the nervous system. Early in my practice, I found when treating headaches that the effect of treatment was far more potent when combining these two tissue salts with vitamin B-complex. The combining of these factors with the herbs for enhanced elimination of toxins has been mentioned in the previous section. The same applies when treating infections. The use of vitamin C and the mineral salts is much more effective when elimination is speeded up through the use of herbs. The final 'icing on the cake' results from the use of the homoeopathic constitutional remedy when indicated.

As an educator in the area of natural therapies I have noted repeatedly that those therapists who combine homoeopathy with herbs, minerals and vitamins are able to cover a far wider range of disorders. Some natural therapists are almost mystically inclined to use only one homoeopathic remedy for each patient without any consideration of first detoxifying the client or treating various deficiencies. These graduates rarely develop large practices and appear to restrict themselves to those idiosyncratic patients who provide classic examples of homoeopathy as it was able to be used 100 years ago. Homoeopathy is of inestimable value however, when used in keeping with twentieth-century needs. The third main internal therapy with a long-standing tradition is therefore homoeopathy. It can be used in a number of ways to complement herbs, vitamins and minerals.

The Principles of Homoeopathy

The founder of homoeopathy, Samuel Hahnemann, was born in 1755 in the town of Meissen, Germany. His higher education was financed by using his extraordinary linguistic talents for tutoring in Greek and Latin and through the translation of English texts into German. He graduated as a Doctor of Medicine from Leipzig. Becoming disillusioned with the medicine of the time, he turned to the translation of medical and scientific works to earn a living. It was during the translation of a treatise by a Scottish physician named Cullen that he decided to investigate the use of Cinchona Bark (quinine) on himself as he was dissatisfied with the dissertation on that medicine. By taking large doses of the extract twice daily he showed that, when given to a healthy person, a drug will produce those symptoms which it is normally given to cure. In other words, Hahnemann developed all the symptoms of malaria. Hahnemann was not the first to discover healing by the law of similars; evidence of this approach is present in the writings of Hippocrates.[16]

Following this discovery, he tested many other substances on himself and others and noted their side-effects were minimised by the use of smaller and smaller doses. The group of people who tested remedies were known as provers and their practice was to take several doses per day of the substance to be tested and to meticulously note all symptoms produced. The common symptoms which all the provers experienced were given more emphasis in the repertory. The first *Materia Medica* was published in 1810 and this volume contained details of every minor and major symptom involving sixty-seven medicines.

Further research was conducted by medical doctors who worked after the death of Hahnemann in 1843. The *Materia Medica* of William Boericke contains provings of nearly 700 substances. Two American doctors, J. T. Kent and C. M. Boger, produced two huge works involving cross-referencing of symptoms and these are known as repertories. They are the bibles of many practising homoeopaths. In these volumes all possible physical, nervous and mental symptoms are correlated with remedies in their order of importance. A practising therapist can therefore look up their patient's symptoms and find all remedies which may be useful for that problem. The final selection from two or three remedies must still be made using the intuitive skill of the homoeopath.

The central tenet of homoeopathic philosophy is the finding that a substance which produces disease symptoms in a healthy person will cure those same symptoms in a sick person. From this clinical finding which Hahnemann first discovered comes the Law of Similars with the consequent catch-phrase 'like cures like'. Homoeopaths who strictly adhere to the classical teaching will search for a single remedy, and will give it in the smallest dose (highest potency) which will stimulate the vital energy in the patient. To develop the system of potentisation, Hahnemann found that the remedy should be divided by diluting to a scaled formula. The decimal (10) and centesimal (100) scales are the most widely used. The potentisation of remedies helps us to understand the possibility of homoeopathy influencing the genetic structures of the cell.

In the case of the centesimal potency, one part of the substance, animal, mineral or vegetable is mixed with ninety-nine parts of the solute, usually alcohol and water. This is sharply succussed (shaken) at least twenty times and the process gives the first centesimal potency. This process is repeated up to a hundred thousand times for the highest potencies. It takes at least 200 dilutions and the accompanying succussion to produce a moderate potency which is suitable for deep-seated problems. In many cases, the therapist will commence with the 200th potency and gradually increase the potency given to the patient, perhaps to the hundred-thousandth potency. After about the 25th decimal potency, according to Avogadro's law there are no chemical molecules remaining. How does the remedy work?

A number of hypotheses have been delineated. Australian medical scientist, Paul Callinan, conducted experiments to show the effect of homoeopathic dilutions on ice crystals.[17] The crystals were found to change their structure in response to dilutions which contained no chemical molecules of the substance.

In Chapter 4, the concepts of Bevan Reid are discussed in relation to homoeopathy. He sees the diluting and succussing process as producing mini pressure waves which provide generations of inducible electron patterns ready to pick up the pattern provided by the drug. In this way the pattern from the remedy substance is imprinted on the solvent. He further suggests that it is a mirror image which is established in the solvent. In other words, the spin of the electrons in the solvent containing the remedy is the reverse of that in the original substance. If this is so, it would perhaps explain the reversing effects which homoeopathic remedies have on illness—the 'like cures like' effect.

Previous models for homoeopathic theory have talked about coherence and resonance. The example of soldiers marching across a bridge could be mentioned here, or the shattering of a glass when a particular note is struck. If the bridge or glass is taken as resembling the disease process, the remedy is the coherent vibration or force as illustrated by the soldiers marching or by the musical note. In either case, the disease (bridge) is destroyed when a particular vibration is sounded. In the case of inherited predispositions (see Chapter 11), if the potentised remedy is given to the patient, we see the possibility of the mirror image of the remedy cancelling out the similar disease pattern in the patient. If the potentising process can influence the electronic configuration of the solution, there is no logical reason why the remedy would not be able to penetrate into the minutest aspect of the cell, thus producing genetic changes.

When preparing homoeopathic remedies from plants, the first dilution is made from the mother tincture which is already a dilution of one in ten. Insoluble substances such as silica, sulphur and carbonates are prepared in the first few dilutions by grinding in a mortar with an inert substance like sugar of milk. Later dilutions are made using alcohol and water. Homoeopathic remedies are used in both liquid and pillule form.

The homoeopathic remedies in low potencies are valuable adjuncts to the herbal toning of organs. A mixture of herbs for the liver in homoeopathic potency of 6 or 12x will therefore be called a liver drainage remedy. The great advantage of using this approach instead of herbal liquid extracts is the ease with which the patient can consume the dose, especially in the case of children, babies or sensitive people. It is easy to disguise a few drops in a drink. There are also particular homoepathic remedies which are amazingly specific for particular conditions. Cocculus Indicus made from the spiral shell of the sea creature who builds the Indian cockle shell is an outstanding example. Remembering the principle of like cures like — the law of similars—one can understand that a remedy made from a structure which goes round and round may be used to resolve giddiness. Such was the problem of Peter who had been flat on his back for five weeks; his case is described in Chapter 10.

The second level of homoeopathic prescribing in our approach is described in the next chapter when examining the chronic miasms. These remedies, which are often nosodes (homoeopathic dilutions of disease processes), are used inter-currently in therapy-resistant patients to clear out blocks caused by inherited disease patterns. The final and most classical approach of constitutional prescribing is appropriate when there has been some detoxification and toning of organs and tissues. These single remedies are selected by taking into account all the idiosyncrasies, both physical and psychological, of the patient. This classical approach, as it has already been called, covers those constitutional, temperamental and environmental factors which make each person uniquely individual.

_____ CASE HISTORIES _____

The two following cases cover the main points mentioned in relation to a synthesis of minerals, vitamins and herbs. The first involved Robert, aged nineteeen, a university student who also does part-time work in sales. He came to the clinic with itching eczema all over the body. The iris (see Chapter 2) revealed a moderately fine blue structure with considerable imbalance in the sympathetic nervous system, moderate lymphatic congestion, and an acid stomach. The condition had been recurrent over a five year period. There were known allergies to pets, petrochemical products, and many other substances.

From the history and iris it was plain to understand that both the allergies and skin rash resulted from particular mineral deficiencies as evidenced by the shape of the 'autonomic wreath' (sympathetic nervous system) in the iris and the congestion of the lymphatic system. As pointed out earlier when discussing allergies, naturopaths are concerned to balance the biochemistry and promote homoeostasis so that the digestive and immune functions are enhanced. This resolves the allergy problem and prevents the social osctracism which would otherwise occur.

The first month of treatment included liver herbs in solid extract and homoeopathic form, lymphatic cleansing herbs, calcium phosphate for the nervous system, and iron phosphate for the inflammation of the skin, vitamin B-complex for general nerve toning and vitamin C to assist the detoxification programme. A homoeopathic antidote to some of the allergies was made and administered. On his return in one month, the skin had improved considerably and sleep was better. The same prescription was repeated, and continued improvement took place. At the third visit, I undertook some allergy testing using the Vega analysis and the following foods were still found to be a problem — peanut butter, Vegemite, yeast, and wheat. As these are a comparatively few items they were then removed from the diet. Skin was very much improved by the next visit and improvement was maintained except when Robert had a binge on pizza and beer before Christmas! This was a good reminder of the dietary factors and he has not succumbed to any temptations in this direction since.

The basic treatment was continued for about nine months and then tapered off to a maintenance dose as a health insurance while under the stress of studying. He can now cope with moderate exposure to pets and petrochemical pollution because the immune system is in a healthier state and the calcium deficiencies have been removed.

This case was chosen partly because it would be almost impossible to isolate any one factor of the treatment as the most important. The synthesis of detoxification using herbs and homoeopathics plus the need for mineral supplementation and the presence of particular vitamins is all illustrated.

At the other end of the scale is a case history involving a synthesis of remedies needed for a chronic situation. Faye first attended the clinic when aged forty-three. She had undergone surgery for a benign tumour of the spine and as a result had difficultly with walking which made her very frustrated. There was a permanent shunt (drainage tube) which had been placed in the skull. She suffered from headaches and considerable irritability before menstruation each month. The diet was good except for chocolate craving before the menstrual period. The bowel was irregular and only worked every three days or so. There were some very large moles on the body which revealed an underlying inherited predisposition towards benign growths. The iris revealed a good basic constitution. It was of interest that her mother had suffered Parkinson's disease, which is a degenerative disease of the nervous system.

The first month of treatment concentrated on the nervous system to improve co-ordination for the walking. To this end, magnesium and potassium phosphate were combined with vitamin B-complex and anti-spasmodic herbs. These same supplements were indicated for the irritability, hypoglycaemia (sugar craving) and headaches. Liver herbs were given for the cleansing and sluggish bowel and zinc was the final mineral needed for a number of signs including the hypoglycaemia, low immunity and nervous irritability. On her return in one month, Faye reported less irritability plus less soreness in the legs. The bowel was not improved. Linseeds were added to the daily regime for the bowel tone and a miasmatic remedy in the form of Thuja 200 was given twice weekly for the moles. At her third visit Faye reported improvement in all respects.

During the next few months improvement was maintained and having just introduced Vega analysis in my practice, this form of evaluation was able to be cross-checked with the iris. The Vegatest indicated that both small and large bowel were still weak in function and there was a pre-malignant tendency revealed in connection with the tumour site. About this time Faye stopped treatment due to financial considerations. From my point of view she should have continued and this may indicate why she returned eighteen months later after a further growth of the tumour for which irradiation was administered. The 'biological age' was moderately high indicating the pathological predisposition in her body. Both the skeletal and the lymph system were involved with her relapse.

Treatment was recommenced with an emphasis on detoxification. Lymphatic cleansing herbs and homoeopathic drainage remedies were combined with the magnesium phosphate, potassium phosphate, potassium chloride and B-complex for the nerves. The Thuja was recommended for the inherited predispositions, and vitamin A added for its preventive care effect on cell membranes. At the next visit Faye reported that she was walking well and feeling good in herself. The potency of the homoeopathic Thuja was increased to the hundred-thousandth (M potency) in an endeavour to control further tumour formation. The other basic treatment was continued and Faye's condition remains stable. She has now agreed that it would be valuable to stay on a maintenance amount of treatment for some time and is prepared to have periodical monitoring at the clinic.

Auxiliary Therapies

It may be useful to describe briefly the other therapies listed earlier so that the reader can understand how these may be applied from time to time in conjunction with the main three internal therapies which have been explored in this chapter. Over the last ten years there has been emphasis on actual body work of many kinds involving chiefly the muscles and meridian system.[18] Acupuncture is the most well known of therapies which involves the meridian system. It uses the basic Chinese medical philosophy which understands that energy balance is a very important aspect of health and healing.

To rebalance the energy of the body needles are inserted at specific locations along energy pathways or channels which are known as meridians. The actual anatomy of these channels is as intricate as Western anatomy and the correlations involve all the organs, tissues and functions of the body. By stimulating or sedating points on the meridians via needles in the skin, body functions are balanced and toxins eliminated. It should be stressed that the traditional Chinese physician often uses herbs and gives counselling on general life-style. Acupuncture is not practised in China in isolation as it often is in the West. The actual needling is therefore an adjunct to the internal therapies already discussed. It is a valuable stimulus for energy balance when used skilfully by a person who has undergone suitable training which must span several years.

A number of other disciplines have developed where the fingers of the therapist replace the needles. These therapies include acupressure, reflexology, Touch For Health, and the dance therapy Tai Chi, where the movements and positions of the dancer are the balancing factors. None of these approaches can replace the detoxification needed by herbs and homoeopathy, or resolve the widespread deficiencies of vitamins and minerals which are found today. They are all valuable aids to the person who has the necessary time, enthusiasm and money.

Massage has also become very popular and more recently, aromatherapy—massage with oils extracted from herbs and flowers—has gained ground. Both these therapies are useful for subclinical conditions as they stimulate blood, nerve and lymphatic channels and therefore assist in the detoxification process. One drawback is that the client usually needs regular weekly treatment for some time before deriving therapeutic benefit. This takes a lot of time and money. Many therapists using these approaches have undertaken their training in a few weekends or week-long seminars and they charge as much as therapists who have undergone full four-year programmes in the main disciplines. The other confusing factor for the public comes from the tendency of these therapists to give the impression that their art covers all that is needed for all health problems.

Longer training and considerable skill are needed in the practice of chiropractic and osteopathy. These are often necessary adjuncts, at least on the first few visits to natural therapists. By balancing the minerals in the body we find the need for osteopathic or chiropractic manipulative treatment is speedily reduced. A number of interesting developments have taken place recently in this area with very gentle techniques involving muscles, and the skeleton is realigned with a minimum of pressure and force. The Bowen technique is one example. Another example involves the Alexander technique where the client is taught to position the head in relation to the spine so that the whole body is realigned. From one point of view it is a form of relaxation, the key phrase being 'allow the neck to be free'. The practice of applied kinesiology is another system where stresses on organs are found by muscle testing and the selection of appropriate remedies is made by the same system.

Meditation is appropriate to mention as basic to any form of healing when considered as relaxation of body, emotion, and mind; and as ideally promoting an alignment with our inner essence or soul—the true healing factor. I am currently working with groups of stressed patients to inspire them to practise daily relaxation, creative visualisation and an alignment exercise where they will invoke healing energies from within themselves on a regular basis. These techniques can also be used to resolve difficult situations at work and in family life. The physical supplements will be much more effective when combined with a meditative approach to life. This area is explored further in Chapter 12.

Psychic healing, magnetic healing, Reiki and spiritual healing are all practised by therapists who use the hands to channel healing energies to the patient. Their success depends on their own inner alignment and spiritual development. They can only channel energies from the subjective level to which they can be attuned. In practice we find that some healers are mainly transmitting the subtle part of the physical plane and they are pranic or magnetic healers. Others work at astral or feeling level and in the case of a pure healer they may be able to be a channel for spiritual or Buddhic energies. Spiritual healing is an unfortunate term as it is used to cover everything which is non-physical and may only mean the astral level which can be far from spiritual. Reiki is another term with little meaning as teachers from different countries make different claims about the level of consciousness they reach, although there is the general agreement of being a channel for healing energies.

All of the therapies mentioned may play a useful part as adjuncts to the main medicinal therapies which involve vitamins, minerals, herbs and homoeopathic remedies. The following case was created to show how some of these other therapies could be integrated with clinical nutrition, herbal medicine and homoeopathy. Such a case may progress as follows.

A middle-aged woman comes to the clinic with the beginnings of arthritis and a general run-down feeling. On questioning it is found that she has little fruit and salad except in the hottest summer months. The long-term approach is therefore to improve her life-style and it is explained that to rebalance the biochemistry, six months of herbs, vitamins and minerals will be used during which time she can gradually change her diet. She is given liver-toning herbs, herbs and a mineral combination to reduce the inflammation of her joints, and a mineral combination and vitamin B-complex for nerve energy. After two months of treatment the joints are considerably improved and dietary changes are under way.

Then a family crisis occurs when her daughter separates from her husband with the result that the client has the children for days on end while the daughter goes out to work. Not only do the joints start to relapse but there is anger and resentment that at her age in life freedom has been curtailed and yet she feels she has to help during this crisis period. At this point flower essences are used to balance the emotions. These are described in Chapter 12. Some counselling is also in order as it becomes obvious that the daughter is manipulating the mother to some extent. If the natural therapist is not able to fulfil this role the patient is referred to a counselling service. It is during this period when emotions come to the surface that the constitutional remedy is noted—perhaps Natrum Muriaticum which corresponds to the nursing of resentment noticed in the client, in addition to other pointers.

Improvement continues and then the client has a fall during window cleaning and injures the muscles and ligaments around the upper spine. She is referred to an osteopath for a few weeks for remedial massage and manipulation of the spine. After eight months of treatment the joints have been free of pain for several months and treatment is tapered off with the proviso that if during winter the aches and pains begin to return she may need a temporary boost. By this time, the daughter has made adequate arrangements for the children while she works and the relationship between mother and daughter has improved as a result of the counselling. The joint stiffness was found to be partly resulting from lack of free flowing creative energy because there were no adequate creative interests. A new start in life is made which accompanies new-found health.

In Chapter 2 we begin to explore the various concepts introduced in this chapter. These ideas include different viewpoints on the subject of vitality, energy and toxaemia.

CHAPTER 2

Vitality and Energy Patterns in Health and Disease

The terms vitality and energy often feature in our language when we feel healthy and have a sense of well-being. If we observe animals and birds in their natural state a sense of strong energy or vitality is often apparent. What is this energy and where does it come from? Where does this energy go when we feel ill and listless? Is the experience of vitality a by-product of good health or is it the basis for health? What does medical science say about the terms energy and vitality?

The Development of the Vitalistic Concept of Medicine

A division between vitalistic and mechanistic thought in medicine existed even before the time of Hippocrates who is generally considered to be the father of modern medicine.[1] With the development of the Hippocratic school, the mechanistic model became gradually accepted as the official medical approach. The contribution of Newton to physics many centuries later underlined the mechanistic model of disease which was viewed as a problem involving one part of the body. Reductionism is an associated term which is commonly used to describe the approach in conventional medicine where health problems are analysed into smaller and smaller parts. Practitioners of natural therapies, on the other hand, have always stressed the need to approach health and disease in an holistic manner.[2]

Modern physics with its emphasis on the relatedness of everything in the universe is able to give meaning to the philosophy and principles associated with naturopathy and natural therapies. Scientists have not yet been able to find an ultimate building block in the universe. The growing understanding of science is that everything in the universe is an expression of energy and this gives a meaningful framework for understanding health and disease in terms of energy.[3]

It is ironic that the early emphasis on a vital force should be vindicated this century by a development in science which is rapidly replacing the reductionist Newtonian approach. Although there seems to be a developing and reasonable scientific explanation for emphasising the role of energy in health and disease, the principles of natural therapy are still sometimes criticised by orthodox medicine for being unscientific. Orthodox medicine, however, is unable to define or measure health or the absence of disease.

The clinical experience of natural therapists demonstrates that the use of vitamins, minerals, herbs and homoeopathy increases the vitality and well-being of the patient. The most common feedback received by thousands of natural therapists is that the clients experience more energy, vitality, and well-being (after participation in a natural therapy programme). The promotion and enhancement of the vital force is understood therefore to be a cornerstone of natural medicine. Later we will explore the idea that there is an underlying aspect of the physical body, which may be described as an energy body, that validates the great emphasis on energy in the practice and principles of natural medicine. During the long development of humanity, we may find in retrospect that the last few decades are comparatively unique in terms of negating the role of energy in medicine. We have only to look at the philosophy of traditional Chinese medicine to realise how well established is the concept of balancing energies for the restoration of health. It is only since the Industrial Revolution, a very short time

The Triangles of Health

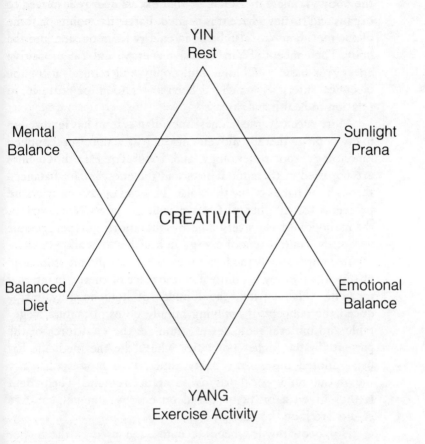

YIN
Rest

Mental
Balance

Sunlight
Prana

CREATIVITY

Balanced
Diet

Emotional
Balance

YANG
Exercise Activity

during our evolution, that the emphasis in health and healing has moved away from the vitalistic concept.

Acupuncture, Homoeopathy and the Vital Force

In the practice of acupuncture, energy in the body is enhanced and balanced by working at sites on the skin called acupuncture points. These are situated on energy channels called meridians which form an interlocking network throughout the body. Generally, needles are used to connect the relevant organs of the body via these meridians so that excess energy is moved to organs and tissues where it is needed. Particular points on some of the meridians can also bring in energy from outside into the body. The concept of Yin (negative energy) and Yang (positive energy) is basic to Chinese philosophy and reminds us of the electrical interplay which has been understood for centuries in relation to health and disease.[4]

More recently, the Chinese meridian system has featured in many popular therapy movements such as acupressure, applied kinesiology, foot reflexology, and Touch For Health. Needles are not used in these modalities and the energies are balanced through the hands of the therapist. This can occasionally create problems for the therapist as we shall see later. Nevertheless, the main point to be stressed here is that more and more people accept the central role of energy in health and healing.

In comparatively modern times, the development of homoeopathy as a therapy has illustrated the place of energy in internal medicine. Hahnemann, the founder of homoeopathy, introduced the concept of applying minute doses of animal, vegetable and mineral remedies to stimulate the vital force of the patient. In the higher potencies where the the medicine has been diluted more than thirty times, it is now statistically shown that no physical original substance remains. The patient is thus given a medicine based on energy and yet curative results are found to take place.[5]

Homoeopathy has been accepted and used in the higher potencies by thousands of medically qualified doctors and natural therapists from Hahnemann's time onwards. As indicated in Chapter 1, laboratory work has shown that the medium in which the homoeopathic remedy is diluted and mixed takes on the electrical pattern of the remedy. Measurements by physicists have been able to show the change of electric configuration in the carrier substance and it is considered that in this way the remedy can influence the energy systems of the body without the presence of any physical molecules in the remedy.

Orthodox medicine does, of course, recognise the close association of energy transformations in every body process. There is however, one particular and main difference in viewpoints. From the orthodox perspective, the energy is seen as an outcome of the chemical and biochemical process rather than as the basis for all the processes. Thus it is accepted that activity in the brain and heart give rise to energy patterns; that the digestive processes produce energy; that the muscles generate activity. However, an underlying energy body is not accepted, nor is the basic need for balancing energies before the digestive system, brain or heart can work adequately. Thus the state of the body is viewed from opposite sides by these two main streams in medicine.

In clinical practice, at the first interview the natural therapist is concerned to establish the energy state of the person. This can be done in a number of ways. The obvious start is the taking of a careful history to establish the life pattern and rhythm of the person. Sleep and eating patterns, digestive function, sexual needs, and psychological states all give important information about energy and vitality. More direct observations are gleaned from pulse diagnosis, dermatoglyphics (skin patterns) and palm print from the hand, and from iris diagnosis, which is the most popular form of analysis used by natural therapists throughout the world.

Iris Diagnosis — A Guide to Vitality

Iris diagnosis is the observation, interpretation and diagnosis of disease from the iris. Reference to changes in the eyes are found as early as in the writings of Hippocrates. The first reference in comparatively recent times is found in the work of Philippus Meyers about the year 1670. The discoverer of the art and science of iridology in its present form was an Hungarian physician, Dr Ignatius von Peczely (1822–1911).[6]

One can view the mechanics of iridology in the following way. The idea of homoeostasis was first introduced by the physiologist Canon in the 1930s. This concept is now explored extensively in modern physiology and indicates that every organ has a functional dependence on every other organ, either directly or indirectly. The homoeostatic mechanism maintains the constancy and balance of the cellular environment, and when disturbed results in abnormal cellular function and finally in pathology. Therefore, any organ of the body will reflect to some extent the state of every other organ. Unless the changes in tissues are extremely pathological, alterations in other organs are only discernible at the cellular level. Hence the blood is often used as the criterion for health in various parts of the body. For an organ to be useful as an indication of physiological health in other organs, several criteria are essential. The organ must have a highly developed vascular and neural supply, must be accessible for easy viewing, and must be structurally or histologically suited for evaluation by a consistent analytical method.

The iris of the eye fulfils all these criteria. Blood vessels form the bulk of the iris so that the vascular supply is extensive. The neural network is very intricate, with numerous nerves coming from the ciliary plexus and forming networks. The iris is also ideal as a basis for evaluation since it is circular and functionally radial. This allows for a circular grid system based on the length of radius and arc of the circle. The precision afforded by this structure is mathematically unique and ideally qualifies the iris for diagnostic purposes.

One of the easiest assessments possible from the study of the iris is the type of constitution possessed by the person in terms of vitality. This is shown in several ways but primarily by the density and shape of the radial iris fibres. Density is classed by some writers in four grades. In the first grade the fibres are close together with no gaps discernible and this corresponds to a good inherited constitution and vitality, and to strong re-cuperative powers. Persons with this type of constitution often push themselves and others hard and can be high achievers due to their inherent energy. Unless their life-style or psychology becomes severely imbalanced, they may only suffer minor health disturbances and tend to respond very quickly to natural therapies. However, it has been noted by a number of natural therapists that cancer cases often fall into this category of iris structure. In other words, when things go wrong for these people they can manifest a negative growth process which corresponds in strength to the basic inherited strong vitality.

The next class of density allows one to see some indication of the next layer of the iris between the fibres. There may be separations between the fibres in some parts of the iris corresponding to weakness in a particular organ. Over nearly two hundred years, iris maps have been correlated with manifested pathology so that modern maps are fairly accurate. Jensen in USA and Deck in Germany have been pioneers in this work.[7] As the fibres become less and less dense in the iris, energy and vitality tend to be less. The autonomic wreath around the pupil (called the collarette in optometry) becomes correspondingly irregular and distended. This wreath is normally one-third from the edge of the pupil and should be a regular, slightly saw-toothed circle. It is found to correspond closely to the state of the autonomic part of the nervous system which is related to all bodily activities not under the control of the will. The shape of the pupil itself also gives a good indication of the balance of the central nervous system, although strictly speaking, this is not part of iris diagnosis.

In those people who, through inheritance and life-style, suffer from poor vitality and recuperative energies, the iris fibres appear like a lace shawl and there is the appearance of many oval shaped lesions which give an indication of which organs in the body are inherently weak. In these cases, treatment will take much longer than in the person with good density of iris fibres. The patient will probably not have a healing crisis or dramatic change in their condition for several months. These patients especially need to be educated from the start as to their constitutional type and potentials.

The iris is, therefore, an excellent guide to the basic energy state of the patient and the expected duration of treatment. If treatment is allowed to run the required course, changes gradually take place in the iris and the density of fibres increases. In the case of the lesions the outline may remain, but within the lesion a number of healing lines appear indicating the improvement of tone in that particular organ. Generally speaking, a poor iris constitution corresponds with the accumulation of toxic waste; this can also be seen in the iris and will be discussed under toxaemia in Chapter 4. The good constitution with high density of fibres indicates a capacity to eliminate toxins efficiently and to manifest a healing crisis which leads back to health.

In the iris of the new-born babe, the fibres are usually fine and close together. The inherited weaknesses often take some months to show and in some cases poor life-style over many years will produce further changes in the iris. In clinical practice we also have the following anomaly. A person born with a good constitution but who develops a poor life-style may suffer from all manner of ailments and become a classic hypochondriac. Conversely, we often find a person who, in spite of a poor inherited constitution and feeble health in childhood accompanying bad diet and mismanagement, develops into a very healthy and well adjusted adult. This is due to a sincere effort to take responsibility for their own health and reminds one of the great importance of psychological balance for good health.

CASE HISTORIES

Will, aged forty-three, has a senior administrative position in the public service. He suffered from general debility, tension headaches, a persistent cough, and at the time of his first visit had symptoms of flu. He also had a small, hard growth near the angle of his jaw which had been there for ten years. His iris was clear blue with fibres straight and moderately dense and this illustrated a basically strong and vital constitution. The autonomic wreath was irregular, indicating the emotional stress and nervous strain which had been present in his life for many years. This strain related to a

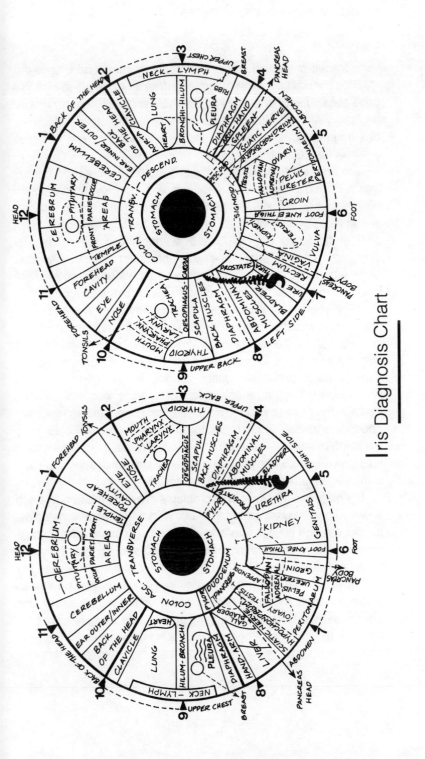

Iris Diagnosis Chart

very difficult marital situation, long hours of study and a stressful, responsible position in the community. In spite of the iris revealing a good constitution, he was temporarily suffering from severe nervous depletion. Although the iris revealed no inherent organ weakness, two major organs—liver and kidney—showed stress via Vega analysis (see Chapter 6).

The first month of treatment was directed to increasing energy with a strong B-complex compound and a specially formulated potassium and magnesium phosphate compound, toning the liver and kidneys with appropriate herbs, and dealing with the current bout of flu using vitamin C and a specially prepared mineral compound of iron phosphate and potassium chloride. Another mineral compound was given to break up the stony lump near the jaw. This mineral tablet contained silica and calcium fluoride.

After one month on this selection of remedies Will had more energy, cessation of headaches, and some elimination through the skin from the lump near the jaw. His cough, largely nervous, still persisted as did a nervous tic near the eye. Readings via the Vegatest had improved as neither liver nor kidneys registered on this second visit. The same selection of remedies was repeated for another two months with the addition of homoeopathic magnesium phosphate in the 30th potency for the nervous tic and cough. By the fourth month Will was feeling very well. Treatment was continued for some months while he sorted out his personal relationships and also took on further responsibilities at work.

For help with the emotional problems involving the family, Bach flower remedies were added. Will also worked on the psychological aspect through counselling and workshops. Eventually he found a more suitable life partner and it was interesting that the more emotional parameters of Will's life were dealt with after his energies and physical well-being had improved. His health has now been stable for many months and only occasional visits for check-ups are necessary. Note that Will had considerable improvement after only one month of treatment and this is in keeping with his iris type.

The next case history is of a different type. Natalie, aged twenty-eight, worked in the area of fashion and was not blessed with a good constitution. Her iris revealed a body laden with toxins in the form of lymphatic congestion, a fairly open iris structure, and inherent weaknesses of the left kidney, the liver and the thyroid gland. According to Vega analysis the liver showed up as the most stressed organ followed by the lymphatic system. The pupil was pulsating when challenged by a strong light which is an indication of the lack of nerve tone plus the need for both magnesium and potassium phosphate.

Natalie felt tired and run-down and her menstrual cycle was very irregular, with periods two to three months apart. She had suffered severe hepatitis at the age of fourteen and had been hospitalised for three months. This was why the liver was still showing up as the most stressed organ, a common finding following hepatitis, despite the fact that the illness may have occurred many years previously. To keep up her flagging energies, Natalie had become a heavy coffee drinker and this further embarrassed her liver and disturbed the blood sugar levels.

The first month of treatment included magnesium and potassium phosphate for energising and balancing the nervous system, vitamin B-complex for energy, calcium phosphate was indicated by the open structure of the iris. Herbs and homoeopathics were administered for the liver, and homoeopathic drops for balancing the endocrine glands which regulate the thyroid and ovaries. After one month on these remedies, her energy improved a little and she had the first menstrual period for some time. The same prescriptions were repeated with the addition of herbal diuretic tablets containing the herb cornsilk. This was to cover oedema in the legs before menstruation and related to the kidney weakness. In the third month an outbreak of herpes occurred and this was treated with homoeopathic Natrum Muriaticum in the 200th potency.

After three months of treatment energy was still a problem although no further herpes occurred. I had already explained to

Natalie that the treatment would take some time because of her particular constitution and she agreed to persevere. The cleansing herbs were changed around and the basic remedies continued with the addition of a zinc compound to improve immunity following the herpes. It was discovered by Vega analysis that pituitary gland function was poor and homoeopathic ammonium carbonate in the 30th potency was given to improve function. In the fourth month Natalie started to feel really good and her improvement continues.

Four months is quite a long time on natural therapies before improvement in energy is noted and in Natalie's case this time factor underscores the individual differences between the vitality factor in different persons. Natalie will probably need another six months of treatment. In her case, the overlap of toxins with the diminished energy levels in the system is obvious from the iris and symptom picture. The hepatitis, although suffered fourteen years prior to naturopathic treatment, caused the system to accumulate toxic waste through a sluggishness of the liver. This had then overflowed into the lymphatic system. The liver has great powers of regeneration and it is surprising how quickly it recovers and gets on with the job of metabolising waste when given a few toning herbs in liquid or homoeopathic form.

The questions may now be asked. If the monitoring and improving of energy is such an important consideration in naturopathic practice, is there any scientific evidence to show that energy or vitality plays a significant role in growth, health and well-being? Can science show that energy disturbances are related to illness and disease?

M edical Science and the Energy Factor

Are there any medical scientists who see energy as a vital factor in health and disease? Are these researchers able to bridge the gap between physics and biology? How do you translate the mystical terms of the vital force of the naturopaths into respectable scientific terminology?

During this century, a number of medical scientists have given credence to the vitalistic concept in medicine. In the main, these outstanding pioneers have been trained in orthodox science and medicine. Yet such is the conservatism of their own professions that usually these people have been ostracised by their peers, and often receive no recognition by the mainstream of medical science. The work of several of these pioneers will now be discussed briefly so that the reader can judge whether the case for a vitalistic force or energy system underlying the physical body is justified.

H. S. Burr and the Life-fields

During the 1940s and 1950s there was the discovery of a bio-electric field with direct current potential pervading the entire organism of living creatures. This field was shown to provide integration and direction for growth processes in the organism.

The field may be described as dipolar, which means that it has a head/tail axis, and it is a summation of the individual fields of all the cells in the organism.

Harold Saxton Burr was one medical scientist involved with this work. Most of his experimental work took place at Yale university where he lectured in anatomy and neurophysiology. His research spanned forty years from 1938 onwards and he published ninety papers during this time. The book *Blueprint for Immortality* summarises this work and the following paragraph is an introductory summary to his concepts about the electrical field interpenetrating the body of living organisms.

> The pattern or organisation of any biological system is established by a complex electrodynamic field which in part is determined by its atomic and physio-chemical components, and in part determines these components in terms of orientation and behaviour. This field is electrical in the physical sense and by its properties, relates the entities of the biological system in a characteristic pattern.[1]

Burr found that his Life-fields had similar properties to simple fields of physics as they could produce an effect across a gap or space. He pointed out that as the measurement could be made a short distance from the skin these fields were not related to surface potential, as for instance in lie detecting. To prevent disturbance of the living system, a special vacuum tube voltmeter was designed. This was necessary because of the tiny voltage gradients involved in these experiments. The Life-field was measured by placing one silver electrode on the forehead and one near the index finger. Alternatively both index fingers were used. A less expensive digital voltmeter is now available for this type of measurement.

In normal persons it was found that the voltage gradients vary over two weekly cycles and this may perhaps relate to the much publicised bio-rhythms. The healthy person has a normal variation which, when graphed, appears as a series of gentle curves over a period of several weeks. There are four categories of persons in terms of voltage patterns with the highest gradient registering at 10 millivolts. The intensity of the field was found to increase sharply during the process of ovulation in mammals. These mammals included monkeys, cats, rabbits, rats and humans. The electrical field of the subject was found to be directly related to the health of organs and cells. The field intensity is greater when we are experiencing well-being and is diminished during states of exhaustion.

Schizophrenic patients exhibit the largest variation in voltage patterns and, to a lesser extent, the pre-adolescent has a field which varies greatly from day to day. In most animals tested the voltage gradients increased steadily during the first third of life, levelled off during the middle-age period and lessened during old age. Following injury and surgery specific voltage patterns were found to manifest. Even small cuts evidenced voltage changes as they healed.

A couple of experiments involving Burr's discoveries are worth briefly relating as they have direct relevance for preventive medicine. At Bellevue State Hospital in New York, Louis Langman, a gynaecologist, screened 1000 women using Burr's technique of Life-field evaluation. The women had been admitted to hospital for a variety of pelvic symptoms. Out of the group, 102 were found to have suspicious voltage gradients and following biopsy, ninety-five were found to have malignant changes.[2] Burr argued that electrical changes in the Life-field take place before pathology is established. He saw the possibility of cheap, effective screening procedures to detect those at risk.

Another well-known experiment involved a small pond creature called a salamander. The salamander egg was measured before fertilisation and then subsequently monitored for the direction of the Life-field. It was found that the longitudinal axis for growth involving the central nervous system was established before fertilisation. This axis did not change direction throughout the entire life of the animal. If similar findings could be established for humans, the health of the child-bearing female, even before conception occurred, would appear to be very important. Any environmental factor which could affect the electrical field may be very significant. One is reminded of the controversy surrounding electromagnetic pollution such as that involving power lines.

Apart from his work with the animal kingdom, Burr undertook extensive research in the vegetable kingdom. The Life-field associated with trees was found to vary with lunar cycles, sunspots, night and day. A synchronicity was established between the tree, earth, air and sunspot activity over a long period of time. In measuring the Life-field of plants, the change of a single gene resulted in considerable change in the voltage pattern. Studies on maize kernels revealed the growth potential of the kernel. It was postulated that using these diagnostic parameters grains and plants could be bred to resist insect infestation.

In a summary of Burr's work, it could be said that Life-fields are found by measuring the difference in voltage between two points on the body. They are described as pure voltage potentials yielding infinitesimal amounts of direct current, independent of current flow and skin resistance, and useful for general diagnostic purposes. The understanding that the electrodynamic fields described may serve as a mould for the growth of physical cells and tissues has direct relevance to preventive medicine. Those therapies which promote the balance and health of the electrical energies and which protect the electrical field from morbid deviations will obviously be important. Later it will be shown that natural therapies profoundly enhance the health and strength of the electrical fields associated with the body.

Further Electrical Models for Growth

Other medical scientists apart from Burr were working during the 1940s and 1950s on electrical fields associated with the physical tissues of living organisms. Gerard and Liber found electrical currents flowing outside the nerve cells in the brain by means of an experiment where, in spite of cut nerve cells placed end to end, a current was still found to flow in the direction of the cut nerves. Chemical transmission between the cut ends was ruled out by placing a saline solution between the ends and observing a subsequent lack of electrical flow.[3]

Dr Robert Becker, a medical scientist researching at the State University of New York, repeated Burr's experiments during the 1960s. He found the electrical field to be more complex than indicated by Burr. Of special importance was his finding that the Life-field related to the nervous system. This was proved by the application of an external current which was able to reverse the usual polarity associated with the nervous system. Becker wrote:

> Evidence is quite conclusive that there are steady DC electrical currents flowing outside of the neurones proper throughout the body. These are non-ionic in nature and similar to semi-conducting type currents. The peri-neural cells appear to be the most likely site at which the currents are generated and transmitted. They constitute a system for transmission of very basic type data.[4]

The last sentence gives the clue to the importance of the electrical or energetic parameters of health and disease. What happens if the wrong data are transmitted? What internal or external conditions may alter the transmission of data, perhaps causing changes which are dangerous for health?

In 1952 a significant experiment was conducted by Beams and Marsh on flatworms. Cut worms in this species usually regenerate with the head up the same end. An external current was introduced to the cut surface to reverse the usual electrical gradient. As the current was increased a head formed at each end of the cut worm, and with further increases in current the head-tail gradient was reversed, indicating that the naturally occurring electrical gradient in this species was capable of transmitting information for growth, i.e. morphological information.[5]

Further valuable information relating disease to electrical changes in the body was revealed through the experiments of

Hasson. Removal of the nerve (denervation) accelerated tumour formation and development from carcinogenic agents. These observations were confirmed in 1967 by Pawlowski and Weddell. Conversely, simulation of nerve supply to the tumour area in mice by the use of copper and zinc anodes for three hours per day was shown to reduce tumours markedly. In other experiments, Huggins and Yang found that carcinogenic agents produce their destructive effects by means of their capacity for electron transfer within cells and tissues.[6] Again, these experiments demonstrate the relation of electrical/energy/nervous stimulus to health and disease.

It appears now that there may be scientific evidence which indicates the relationship between electrical fields associated with the body, the nervous system and immunity. Although cancer may be the most dramatic example of electrical imbalances, an enormous range of disease processes could be similarly affected. For many years naturopaths have stressed the importance of enhancing energy and vitality in the body through the use of correct nutrition, life-style and the use of supplements such as vitamins, minerals, herbs and homoeopathy. They have understood that a close relationship has always existed between the immune system and energy levels in the body.

Burr's work gave us the concept that the direction for growth and development is given by the electrical field and that changes in this field precede both normal growth and development. In the experiments by Beams and Marsh we have seen that the electrical field is able to transmit information for growth. These concepts are an echo of Eastern teachings about health and disease. Such philosophy has always discussed energy fields as being the substance underlying the material universe of both animate and inanimate objects.

The influence of electromagnetic fields on living tissue is further indicated in the following experiments. In 1950 Singer showed limb regeneration in the salamander to depend on the presence of a small amount of nerve tissue in the amputation stump. In regenerating animals such as the salamander, after injury there is a positive electrical potential for three days and then a negative potential which coincides with blastema formation. The blastema is a primitive stage of cell formation from which other more specialised cells can develop. In non-regenerating animals, such as mice and men, there is no blastema formation following injury and hence, under normal circumstances, limbs and parts cannot regenerate.

Becker asked whether regeneration of a limb could take place if blastema formation was simulated in a non-regenerating animal by a negative electrode placed near the amputated stump. In 1972 he achieved regeneration of a forearm in a rat by implanting suitable electrodes in the amputation stump. In 1982 Rose showed that regeneration could take place in the salamander after the nerves had been removed from the forelimbs provided there was daily application of negative polarity to the stump. The information for growth appeared to be stimulated by the negative potential and to depend on the junction between the nerves and the skin—the neuro-epidermal junction. Becker writes in summary of this concept: 'The specific sequence of changes in electrical potential that produce regenerative growth are produced by the neuro-epidermal junction and not by nerves or epidermis alone . . . Intrinsic electromagnetic energy in the nervous system is the factor that exerts the major controlling influence over growth process in general'.[7]

To summarise the work of Becker and other scientists working along similar lines: according to Becker there is a type of data transmission taking place in the body which, again according to Becker, is present in solid state electronics. Certain structures in the body have a crystalline or lattice-type structure which stores and transmits data for growth and regrowth. Examples of such structures have been found to be peri-neural tissue and bones. These findings validate the concern which natural therapists have for maintaining the electrical integrity of the body through good life-style and by therapies which enhance and promote vitality and energy. It appears that changes in energy states which relate to growth, and hence also to health or disease, have been demonstrated by a number of scientists using electrical parameters. The relationship of these changes to growth and development has been indicated. A more pictorial method of indicating the electrical parameters of health and disease has been developed using high frequency photography.

Energy States and Photography

Any object placed in an intense electrical field will radiate a charge producing the phenomenon of a corona around the object. This was first noticed around the masts of sailing ships in thundery weather and was called St Elmo's fire. The phenomenon results from high voltage ionising gases in the air and is sometimes termed coronal discharge. To capture the image on a photographic plate no external light source is needed and the photograph results from the electrical discharge between the plates acting as electrodes.

The possibility of using the technique in medicine was first developed in 1939 by a Russian medical researcher, Semyon Kirlian. He was holding a photographic film in an operating theatre when his hand accidentally became exposed to a volley of electrical sparks from a diathermy machine near by. On developing the film for routine purposes, a photograph of the hand was found.

The basic equipment used in the process is a high-frequency generator controlled by special timing circuits. The power source is connected directly to a metal electrode which is covered by a smooth-fitting dielectric sheet such as plate glass. Film is placed on the electrode and the recording of the subject is captured by still photography, video or direct viewing.

Provided the electrical parameters of the photography remain constant, the photograph of inanimate objects such as coin, jewel or rock remains the same. In living subjects the patterns change according to health, well-being and disease.

Various observations by a number of medical scientists have indicated that diagnosis can be made about the state of health in the plant, animal or human using this form of photography.

In Roumania, a medical scientist named Dumetrescu photographed acupuncture points to aid in the diagnosis of incipient colitis and ulcers. An American medical researcher, Leonard Konikiewicz, correctly identified cystic fibrosis in 90 per cent of cases submitted as photographs. In the vegetable kingdom, the health of a shrub was able to be identified from photographs of a single leaf.

In the 1970s one of the leading researchers in this area was the American psychologist Thelma Moss.[8] She was particularly interested in isolating the factors which produce the picture. Experiments were conducted to establish whether the corona around living objects was changed through the amount of sweat, heat or coldness of the skin, or through the psychological state of the person. It was found that the degree of relaxation in the subject was the most influential factor in producing a wide, even corona around the fingertips. The colour changes were finally traced by later researchers not to the amount of sweat, but to the type of electrolyte (salt) in the sweat. This was found to alter according to the type of disease.

In the case of rheumatoid arthritis the disease was found to give a typical snowflake pattern. There are 300 sweat glands on each fingertip. The transport of sodium, potassium, and chloride ions across the cell membranes is involved. Sweat secretion is related to vasomotor activity and this is further locked into spinal and cerebral factors. Further factors have been found to include any drugs or chemicals consumed. The coronal discharge images of the fingertip reflect objectively the equilibrium state of the homoeostatic mechanisms operating at the time of photography.

Some medical researchers have found the fingertip luminosity to vary cyclically and in the female this was found to coincide with the menstrual cycle. In cancer cases, this cyclic activity was found to be replaced by a continuous luminosity.

This recalls the work of Burr who found that the electrical field intensity of the subject also had an ebb and flow over several weeks. After successful surgery for cancer, the cyclic pattern of the aura again became apparent in photographs.

Some people have mistakenly claimed that this form of photography captures the auras seen by clairvoyants. There may be some relationship but it needs to be remembered that high-frequency photography is a physical phenomenon which translates the biological state of the subject photographed into electrical parameters. The clairvoyant is more likely to be observing the subjective states lying below or beyond the subtle physical changes in the electromagnetic field of the patient. It has been observed that some people can alter their coronas at will by controlling their thoughts. Some of these results have been recorded pictorially in *The Living Aura* by Kendall Johnson.[9] The old adage of energy following thought is thus illustrated and will be explored more fully in a later chapter. The relation between our psychological state and electromagnetic field appears to be very intimate.

So far we have examined energy in terms of electromagnetic fields associated with the body, but where does this energy come from? Is there a state of energy behind the electromagnetic fields? What is the pattern behind the field which directs the de-differentiated cells of the amputation stump to form the limb correctly? We know that each cell has in its molecules the blueprint for all our development, but in the case of regeneration what provides the pattern?

Physicists have found that space is not empty but full of energy. Eastern philosophers have told us for thousands of years that there is a universal energy which pervades and substands all manifestation in our everyday world. Living organisms are therefore not isolated from each other but may perhaps be profoundly influenced by many types of energy changes in the environment. The work of Rupert Sheldrake, a young scientist in the United Kingdom, has raised a storm of controversy in the area of biology and other overlapping disciplines.

The Morphogenetic Fields of Sheldrake

Sheldrake has undertaken work which appears to vindicate the older philosophical view of a field called 'ether', which not only unites all manifestations in the universe but which provides the pattern and receptacle for growth and knowledge. In his book *A New Science of Life* he writes:

> Specific morphogenetic fields are responsible for the characteristic form and organisation of systems at all levels of complexity, not only in the realm of biology, but also in the realms of chemistry and physics. These fields order the systems with which they are associated by effecting events which, from an energetic point of view, appear to be indeterminate or probalistic; they impose patterned restrictions on the energetically possible outcomes of physical processes . . . the hypothesis is concerned with the repetition of forms and patterns of organisation; the question of the origin of these forms and patterns lies outside its scope.

Sheldrake has gone one step further than those physicists who have explained the universe as a sea of energy from which all forms can be derived and reduced. He has postulated the link between energy and form in the concept of a field which provides the pattern for all things animate and inanimate. Furthermore, this field includes not only the pattern for physical form but the transmission of psychic and psychological data:

> If an animal, say a rat, learns to carry out a new pattern of behaviour, there will be a tendency for any subsequent similar rat to learn more quickly to carry out the same pattern of behaviour . . . if the speed of learning of rats in another laboratory, say in New York, were to be measured before and after rats in London were trained, the rats tested on the second occasion should learn more quickly than those tested on the first.[10]

Sheldrake appears to be making an important contribution which links the world of the physicist with the world of the biologist, as well as placing in a scientific context the metaphysical teaching of the East about the etheric level of the physical plane. These changing viewpoints within science about the universe and biological growth have significant implications for physiology, health and disease, and are a move in the direction of understanding the etheric mechanism as the vehicle for transmitting the pattern for growth in health and disease.

Bevan Reid, an Australian scientist, has also explored the gap between the world of physics and biological processes. Like Sheldrake's, his work goes beyond the electromagnetic fields of Burr and Becker. Reid moves into a formless realm which provides the patterns for growth and development at the junction where ether and the material world meet.

CHAPTER 4

Etheric Energy, Science and Medicine

Is there a possibility that Eastern philosophers have been closer to understanding the creation of our physical world than has modern science? Is the concept of an etheric realm underlying the manifestation of the physical world and all living creatures about to gain scientific validity and understanding?

Bevan Reid and the Revival of Ether as a Primary Force

Reid is a graduate in both veterinary and medical science. Since 1952 he has lectured to medical students and graduates at the University of Sydney. His research, mainly in the area of oncology (cancer research), during this period has been published in almost one hundred articles in scientific journals. He has won international prizes for cancer research. His most controversial research has taken place in the 1980s and has extraordinary implications for biology and medicine. Most of this work is yet to be published.

Action at a Distance. The concept of action at a distance is not yet accepted by many scientists. If this concept is true it means that the growth and biochemisty of

53

living organisms may be profoundly affected by electromagnetic and chemical changes taking place in the near environment. Furthermore, this finding has led to new ideas about the creation of matter and the development and growth of living organisms. There are important implications for health and disease.

Reid first noticed the phenomenon of action at a distance through observations of crystals growing in his laboratory.[1] Sodium chloride crystals were found to develop into rhomboidal forms with branching structures instead of the expected cubic form. Such a phenomenon normally only happens in the presence of albuminoid matter. The branching effect took place as a result of an interaction through space with other experiments undertaken many metres away. Significant effects came from nearby laboratory work involving substances with a lattice-type or repetitive structure such as ice, lead, rubber and silicic acid. The highly ordered or latticed arrangement in these substances appears to amplify energies and assist in transmission through space.

The first observation involving action at a distance related to branching effects in crystals as a result of an experiment taking place next door where a scientist was using silicic acid. The structure of this acid involves the repetitive pattern previously mentioned. At any point Reid was able to tell whether this acid was being employed next door by observing the growth of his crystals. In other experiments, the effect of lead at a distance was observed. A lump of lead near crystals caused a diffraction pattern and the effect continued when the lead was moved far enough away to discount any electromagnetic effect. Any substance with a repeating structure was found to give this effect of action at a distance.[2]

Following the work on crystals was the effect of action at a distance involving bacteria. The effect on cells through space from the drug Colchicum was noted. Firstly, cells were inoculated with the drug and died. Then nearby uninoculated cells died in spite of the barrier from their quartz or glass containers. The Colchicum was moved further away to discount any electromagnetic transmission. The cells still died. In another experiment with a similar sequence of events, uninoculated cells died from as far away as the next building when the drug Vinblastine was used to inoculate a culture.

The finding that space also has a memory and can store information for several months is even more controversial than action at a distance. That space has a memory was discovered by chance when Reid noticed a blue patch of copper sulphate crystals amongst sodium chloride crystals. No laboratory work had been done with the former salt for several months. He concluded that the laboratory space (ether) had been imprinted by the copper sulphate during experiments using this salt and the resulting imprint was able to influence subsequent experiments. The presence of copper was shown by a histo-chemical test involving Haematoxylin.

The Vortices of Ether. To store the records of copper on the slides, Reid covered them with a thin layer of polystyrene. When focusing the microscope through the polystyrene layer it was discovered that energy patterns in the form of vortices appeared to be imprinted in the polystyrene. This phenomenon was later deliberately used to capture the energy patterns of the laboratory space and thus to have a permanent record. For this purpose, the slides were covered with a thin, drying layer of liquid polystyrene at the same time as the experiments on crystal growth took place. The finding of vortices in such space opened up a new line of speculation about the relation between energy and matter. Action at a distance ceased to be an isolated phenomenon and gave way to concepts about the formation of matter and how the energies intrinsic to space may influence biology, physiology, health and disease. The vortices accidentally noted in the polystyrene coating began to reveal themselves as intimately related to the structuring of matter and thus to patterns of growth.

An important associated parameter for the manifestation of the vortices was minute fluctuation in atmospheric pressure. These changes were recorded by an aneroid micro-barometer and variations of 0·1 to 0·3 mm of mercury occurred during action at a distance, as distinct from normal background fluctuations of 0·01 to 0·1 mm of mercury. The minute changes in pressure were associated with the appearance of the microscopically visible vortices on the polystyrene-coated slides. During experiments, the number of vortices increased from one or two per slide, as found with normal background readings, to ten or twenty per slide. In other words when something is happening to matter, lots of vortices appear.

Vortices are considered to be carriers of information due to their unique structural features. Reid and associates created an artificial vortex on polystyrene with two electrodes of known voltage difference for purposes of calibrating the natural space vortices. The distance between the successive spirals of known voltages of a vortex was measured. It was then possible to compare these measurements with the same distance in the naturally occurring vortices found in free space which can be imprinted on the polystyrene. Values of 1·5 to 3·5 millivolts per millimetre were found and these compare with the energy potential of living cells.

At this point, the model of the ether force which Reid has developed can be briefly described. This model involves a continuous flow of energy in and out of matter. Changes of pressure engender a front or 'edge' which in turn causes a stacking or collimating of vortices. The very structure of the etheric force of Reid is vorticeal. The vortices are the elements of the formative process in nature. Mathematically, a vortex continues to infinity and this implies continuous creation and flow of energy.

Vortices and Differentiation of Matter

Reid believes that the vortices are behind the creation of the electron which is presently the most basic unit of matter which can be demonstrated by science. He conceives of the electron appearing as a result of enormous pressure from the ether as it moves through a crevice or 'nozzle' provided by the spaces of the proton lattice within the atom. Local energy concentrations can occur when energy passes through a nozzle and this concentrated jet of energy can be shown mathematically to contain the energy necessary to create an electron. In this instance, there is a manifestation of coherence in terms of the stacking of etheric vortices and by means of pressure through the 'nozzle', a differentiation in the form of electrons takes place.[3]

Reid sees the cycle of creation and maintenance of healthy growth in the body as involving a balance between turbulence and coherence. This is similar in a way to the philosophy long held by naturopaths. The two poles are envisaged as sclerosis (extreme coherence), as occurs in cancer, and inflammation or fever (turbulence). It is well documented that if a fever can be induced in a cancer patient, the tumour may disappear. This subject is explored in Anthroposophical medical literature and is practised in European clinics which follow that particular medical approach.[4]

Reid's theory may explain this clinical phenomenon in terms of physics and bio-physics. He sees normal growth taking place when energy moves from the etheric realm into the world of physics and differentiates to form electrons and then the atoms, molecules and forms with which we are familiar. The original impetus for this creation comes from the collimation of vortices. If differentiation stops taking place in the cellular world the same collimating effect can be seen in the wrong place, for instance in the tissue changes of arthritis or cancer. Some form of turbulence through heat, sound, or even meditation may break up this coherence and then redifferentiation or normal growth returns. The process may be illustrated by the familiar example of soldiers marching across a bridge. To prevent the collapse of the bridge, the coherence is abolished by the soldiers breaking step (turbulence).

Reid visualises continuous interaction between space and matter. The etheric outflow from matter manifests as an exact copy of the form it has taken from matter, including all structural details. For example, the bacterial image in the polystyrene, a particularly inert substance, takes up the same stain as the real bacteria. The inflow may carry instructions for the pattern of a growing structure such as the crystals in Reid's experiments or the tip of a biosystem. This recalls the work by Becker where the cathode electrode simulating a neuro-epidural junction was able to to carry information for the regeneration of a stump in animals.

Reid sees space as a vehicle for energy replicas or exact images of living organisms. Conversely, the vortices appear to carry information for growth and biochemical changes and they may be the energy behind every living cell. Is the vortex the fundamental energy pattern which Eastern philosophers have said carries the patterns for all manifestation in the physical universe? Are these small vortices in space the carriers of all information for the growth and structure in living organisms?

The Spiral or Vortex in Nature and Art

The spiral and logarithmic properties of vortices is the spiral form that is a basic pattern which is repeated in nature, architecture and art. Leonardo Fibonacci was one of the greatest mathematicians of the Middle Ages and he rediscovered the simple number sequence the basis for the mathematical ratios involved with a spiral. The Fibonacci sequence is 1, 1, 2, 3, 5, 8, 13, 21, 34, 55, and so on to infinity. The reader will note that each successive number is derived by adding the previous two digits. The ratio of any number to the next higher is approximately ·618 to 1 and to the next lower number 1·618 to 1. This is known as the Golden ratio or Golden mean and is an important factor in the logarithmic spiral.[5]

This Golden ratio has been noted in the paintings of Leonardo da Vinci, the geometry of Pythagoras, proportions of the great pyramid of Gizeh, Greek temples, snail shells, sunflowers, and in the eight-note octave of Western music. The logarithmic spiral which develops from this particular ratio has no boundaries and is a constant shape. In fact, it is the only spiral that never changes its shape. The centre is never met and the outward reach is unlimited. The vortices of space discovered by Reid have the same mathematical composition as the logarithmic spiral noted in nature and art. Could the vortex be a pattern which is a precursor for physical matter in all its states and evolutionary development?

Reid has gone one step further towards the energy which creates the electromagnetic field and which at the same time carries the information pattern for the form of growing structures. The electromagnetic field associated with living organisms is thus seen by him to result from the patterned energy as it produces growth or regeneration. He comments that matter in itself appears to be inert and energy is the fashioning agent. Once fashioned, the structure can have a reflex action on the energy field by which it is created and with which it is subsequently permeated. This is the viewpoint held by most esotericists who have studied Eastern philosophy and who accept the concept that there is an energy body which substands every part of the physical body and which is the determining factor in health and disease. This energy or etheric body will be explored in Chapter 10.

Of special interest is the proposal by Reid as to a cycle of creation which involves the following chain: pressure changes (a 'sheer' or 'front' resulting in collimation or stacking of the vortices), then the forcing of this energy through a nozzle to imprint and to create electrons and thus matter. Mathematical calculations showed that these jets of energy could either create an electron or alter its cloud structure around the atomic nucleus. This may explain the observed change in electrical parameters of solutions involved in his experiments and could be responsible for the successful preparation of homoeopathic remedies through diluting and shaking. The shaking would produce mini pressure waves which in turn would imprint inducible electron patterns strictly in the pattern of the remedy.

The homoeopathic principle may be only the vanguard of a

cavalcade of phenomena of benefit to clinical medicine which may follow a clearer understanding of the relations between subtle energy forms and matter.[6] The main implications for medicine and health from Reid's discoveries are as follows. Biological systems are not isolated but are connected by means of ether through space (action at a distance). This ether force has a patterning effect on all matter—animate and inanimate (vortices carry information). If there is an interruption to the flow of energy in and out of matter there may be a disturbance to the normal pattern and disease can occur (coherence and turbulence). Cancer is an extreme example where energy is in a state of extreme coherence caused by etheric forces having incorrectly patterned physical matter. As Eastern philosophers have taught for centuries, the energy pattern underlying the physical body is responsible for health or disease.

The findings of Bevan Reid may partly explain the clinical work of therapists who are working in this field of bio-energetic medicine and who use a range of electronic instruments to monitor energy states in the patient which correspond to health or disease.

CHAPTER 5

Using Bio-energetic Medicine

The balance of energies associated with bodily health is intrinsic to the understanding and practice of natural therapies. These energies are seen as the cause of health or disease and not as a by-product of physiological processes. A few scientists have done research which tends to validate the concept that changes in energy patterns associated with the physical body underlie disease patterns. If energies are so important in health and disease, have science and technology developed any instrumentation to measure energies in keeping with naturopathic practice?

Until recently, evaluation of body energies took place by means of inference on the part of the therapist, following general observations and physical examination which often included iris diagnosis. There was no specific means for evaluating energy in, for instance, electrical terms. In an age of technology it was only a matter of time before such instrumentation would be developed. Appropriately, just as the practitioners of Chinese medicine and philosophy were the first to accept the basis of energy balance as intrinsic to health, they were also the first to use instruments to measure the electrical parameters of the body in clinical practice.

Diagnosis through Bio-energetic Evaluation

In the last four decades a new form of patient evaluation has developed, based on the concept that energy disturbances take place before and accompany all disease states. The first group to accept and use this technology were the acupuncturists and they developed simple devices to measure skin resistance at acupuncture points for purposes of locating and validating the existence of these points.

The next step was to establish a correlation between the various acupuncture meridians and points and traditional Western anatomy and physiology. A number of research studies, especially those by the German medical doctor and acupuncturist Reinhold Voll, have correlated electrical disturbances at acupuncture points with faulty physiology and pathology and with the traditionally associated organs and organ function. These studies have only become possible with the advent of bio-energetic medicine of which Voll was one of the earliest pioneers.[1]

Instruments were developed to measure the difference in skin resistance between acupuncture points belonging to different meridians. This gave an indication of energy imbalance between organs associated with each meridian. A further development saw the introduction of remedies by Voll into the 'circuit' between patient and machine so that the energic effect of the remedy on the organ was evaluated via changing readings of skin resistance.

The latest form of bio-energetic evaluation to emerge is known as Vegatesting and this was developed in 1970 by Helmut Schimmel, a German graduate of medicine, dentistry, and naturopathy. Schimmel was using Bio-Functional Diagnosis (BFD) which developed from the work of Voll. This system involved the use of dozens of measurements on different acupuncture points and a therapist would take considerable time to evaluate each patient. Such an approach required detailed knowledge of the Chinese meridian system by the operator. The complexity of the system caused Schimmel to investigate the possibility of a simplified approach.

Schimmel reasoned that by introducing homoeopathically prepared ampoules of organ tissue into the circuit it might be possible to use only one acupuncture point. Instead of changing the points, the ampoules were changed. After a few early difficulties, Schimmel found this system to be vastly superior in terms of time-saving and clinical usefulness. It is a very open ended system as there is no limit to the types of substance that can be introduced for evaluation or to its ability to determine compatability or allergic reaction on the part of the patient to a particular substance or remedy. An instrument was then devised to accommodate the introduction of ampoules into the circuit for evaluation, diagnostic purpose and remedy selection. Some thousands of physicians in Europe now use this system for both diagnosis and selection of compatible treatment.[2]

At this point, we are mainly concerned with principles and how this form of diagnosis fits with the previous discussions about change of energy in health and disease and with transmission of information about energy states in health and disease. How does this form of bio-energetic diagnosis work? From the physical point of view it is based on a Wheatstone bridge, which is a simple but accurate means of measuring skin resistance. Changes in pressure on the probe or electrode used and the amount of sweat on the skin can affect the readings. The aim is to apply consistent parameters so that comparative readings between meridians or between ampoules may be obtained.

Subjective Factors in Vegatesting. There is however, another factor to consider. The subtle or subjective factor has been found to be very significant in Vegatesting. For example, results will vary depending on whether or not the operator concentrates on the particular organ or test sample concerned. It is therefore difficult to present Vegatesting as a completely objective analysis when used in its most common mode. On the other hand, two therapists correctly using the technique have been found to get consistent results. The input from the therapist is thus critical and the circuitry of the instrument appears to be a focusing mechanism for the therapist. The fact that it is not always an objective evaluation does not mean that it is not a valuable technique. We need however, to explore how the subjective factor between therapist and patient may work.

Once again we are observing action at a distance. How does information from the organs of the patient travel along the simple one-volt circuitry of the instrument to the therapist? How is it that some experienced therapists can use the instrument adequately without any ampoules connected, and get the same results as when they put the ampoules in the circuit? Why is it that some therapists are unable to use the instruments no matter how well they are motivated? Are we looking at a type of radiesthesia based on the extra-sensory faculty of clairsentience, which means the touching or feeling of energies?

It appears that the thoughts and attitude of the therapist may be important and may influence the results. Perhaps the energy interaction between the therapist and patient transmits the information from the patient to the therapist, provided the therapist tunes in deliberately on the patient. This information may then register via the electromagnetic field of the therapist to the electrical circuitry of the instrument.

A further clue may be given in the research which has been done on magnetic crystals situated near the pineal gland deep within the brain. The first work done on these crystals took place in birds and fish and accounted for their sense of direction and migratory patterns.[3] This research has now been extended to humans and indicates conclusively that humans also have a magnetic sense.

The amplification effect of certain substances whose molecules are arranged in columns or chains such as ice, lead, and rubber has already been mentioned. Crystals are another good example of this effect and as magnetic crystals exist in the human brain, they would have an amplifying effect. By concentrated thought and through focusing information from the patient, this information could then be transmitted via the energy field and nervous system of the operator to influence the circuitry of the diagnostic equipment.

Objective Forms of Bio-energetic Diagnosis

The various diagnostic instruments on the market can be used in a more objective manner by measurement of the level of energy flowing through any meridian. Examples are the Dermatron, an instrument developed from the work of Voll, the Theratest which relates to Bio-Functional Diagnosis, and the Vega which can also be used in an objective mode.[4] For this form of evaluation, an accurate knowledge is needed of acupuncture points on the meridian selected.

The manufacturers of Vega have also produced an instrument known as the Segmental Electrograph and this instrument provides a completely objective analysis of function related to the various segments of the body. The final differentiation of problems within those segments must be evaluated using standard Vegatesting techniques. Further research at Heidelberg University in West Germany is developing a very objective form of energy evaluation based on fibre optics.

The more subtle factors will relate to the actual relationship between the therapist, probe or electrode, and patient, and involves also the controversy of whether energy channels such as meridians exist at all.[5] An additional query is what level of energy in a specific meridian is the right amount? To overcome this problem it is generally agreed that the main criterion for diagnosis is to find which meridians and their associated organs have less or more energy than the others. The remedies used will be those which bring the meridians and thus, organs and tissues into balance with each other. This has certainly been the overall aim of all natural therapists—that is, to balance the energies in the whole system.

Due to the lower cost and greater flexibility of Vegatesting, this instrument has become the most popular instrument on the market in Europe and the United Kingdom. The very specific and useful information which this instrument delivers is concurrent with an emphasis on the input from the therapist. Some people have used the findings of quantum physics to illustrate and validate the relationship between the energy field of the therapist and patient. This undeniable fact can perhaps be taken too far if it is used as an excuse for excessive variability between the findings of one therapist and another. It has already been mentioned that consistency between therapists has been observed, although it remains for acceptable research to be undertaken in this area. Clinical trials of this nature are under way at Heidelberg University.

A Model for Vegatesting. Due to the popularity of Vegatesting, a possible model for its *modus operandi* has been devised, based on the suggestions in the previous paragraphs. There is a circuitry which carries one volt and which links patient, test ampoules and therapist. The electrode held by the therapist measures skin resistance over a particular point, and an acupuncture point on the end of a finger or toe is usually selected. An assessment is made by the therapist to gauge whether this is a suitable point. This means that the energy manifesting through this point must be demonstrated as responding to test ampoules placed in the circuit. Usually a test ampoule containing some substance inimical to life is placed in the circuit and the typical response by the indicator of the instrument is known as an indicator drop. Once this has been achieved, the operator knows that this point can respond to a challenge from any organ samples, drugs, allergens or remedies placed in the circuit.

At this point in the procedure, an interesting observation underlines the subjective input from the operator. Provided the skin surface remains fairly constant in terms of moisture, and provided the pressure of the probe on the skin remains constant, one would expect uniform results with the procedure. This is not so. Firstly, it takes some therapists months to master the technique in spite of learning to keep a constant pressure fairly easily. Secondly, I have observed that when the test ampoule is inadvertently left in the circuit, no 'indicator drop' occurs, even when the test ampoule is a poisonous substance.

It appears that there must be some concentration by the therapist on the substance, organ or remedy in the circuit before the circuitry can respond with a reading. Perhaps the operator bridges the gap with his or her consciousness between the substance in the test ampoule and the actual electrical circuit. In this way the circuit can be understood as a carrier wave for the test substance and its effect on the patient by the thought process of the operator. Before the reader dismisses this model as too nebulous for consideration, they should be reminded that in spite of these observations, there has been consistency in diagnosis between operators. The subjective factor or intuitive faculty which seems to be involved does not mean, therefore, that the process is not valuable for diagnosis.

The factors involved are the circuit between patient, test sample and therapist, plus the connecting thought process of the therapist. Experienced therapists have found that once they have used a set of test ampoules for a while, they can obtain the same diagnostic results without actually placing them in the circuit, but simply by concentrating on the substance to be tested in relation to the patient. In other words, the therapist is able to use his or her energy field to link with the energy field of the patient and express the findings through the measuring device of the instrument. It is quite likely that the magnetic crystals in the brain of the therapist act as amplifiers for the information received which is then transmitted to the instrument through the energy field and nervous system of the therapist.

Radionics and Vegatesting. The whole process has been exhaustively discussed in radionic literature and the reader is referred to the great deal of experimental and clinical literature on this subject.[6] The main difference between the practice of radionics and Vegatesting lies in the greater use of actual test samples by the latter, whereas in radionics the organs and remedies are assigned 'rates' which are depicted by a number for the vibration of everything to be tested. Radionics has therefore a more abstract or greater subjective factor.

Radionics is based on the premise that energy follows thought and the operator tunes into the energy fluctuations of the patient in health and disease. All diseases have been assigned a rate and the sample of hair or blood from the patient is matched against various rates which are dialled on an instrument. The operator asks questions about the sample and records the answers by means of a pendulum or instrument which records the changes in the energy field of the therapist who is asking the question.

Vegatesting is a more direct and sophisticated way of obtaining the information from the patient. The question is implied rather than directly asked and this may be preferable because it relies less on the psyche of the operator. The use of actual test samples and the physical presence of the client make error less likely. This brings us to some important considerations.

At the time of writing, the use of electronic diagnostic instruments still involves a minority of practitioners. There has been an enormous acceleration of interest in the subject over the last two or three years. This is partly due to the considerably improved clinical results as experienced by both therapists and their patients. It is expected that there will be a rapid explosion of interest over the next ten years to the extent that the public may expect a natural therapist to use such a means of diagnosis.

A very real danger exists for the future of natural therapies because untrained people are buying instruments, believing that they do not need any academic knowledge of pathology or remedies because the instrument is capable of infallible information. Unlike the orthodox medical profession, any lay person has access to the products from manufacturers of these instruments. Short seminars by representatives of some manufacturers are regularly attended by lay people who then have ready access to such machines. This situation reflects adversely on well-trained therapists who, due to their knowledge of anatomy, physiology and pathology and methods of treatment, have a reference point for any diagnosis and remedy selection made by an instrument. In this setting, dangers from the subjective factor are minimised and an approach such as Vega-testing becomes a valuable addition to the other skills of the therapist. Some case histories will be given in the next chapter to illustrate the extra dimension which such testing can give in addition to history-taking, observation, palpation and more usual assessments.

CHAPTER 6

Practical Applications of Bio-energetic Medicine

There is a great emphasis among all kinds of practitioners for evaluating energies. What conditions can bio-energetic instruments monitor? Can this type of evaluation help with the identification of allergies and some of the strange new ailments which result from chemical and electromagnetic pollution and from Geopathic stress?

Examples of Vegatesting

Identifying allergies has become an obsession of the 1980s. It is true that due to the many thousands of chemicals to which we are exposed, allergy and sensitivity problems have greatly increased. The poor life-style of many people also renders them more vulnerable to foreign substances as a result of lowered immunity. This subject will be fully examined in the next chapter. The naturopathic viewpoint has always been that by increasing immunity through healthy organ function, allergies tend to disappear.

However, both patients and physicians may need to discriminate between hundreds of possible allergens, so bio-energetic instruments can save enormous amounts of time. When used correctly there can be very accurate in diagnosis of allergies and allergens. This form of diagnosis and assessment

70

eliminates the need for time-consuming patch or blood tests or the more uncomfortable process of fasting for days before a 'challenge' with the suspected substance. In the space of an hour, by using Vegatesting one can check several hundred allergens on the patient by placing the test substance in the circuit and noting the reaction by means of the indicator.[1]

Once again, the integrity of the therapist is all-important as false results can be obtained. I have been consulted by patients who have brought enormous lists of supposed allergens and whose diet has been reduced to a few items so that life has become totally devoid of culinary pleasures. Why is common sense so rare? Conversely, it is true that a few persons have become so debilitated in their digestive capacity and immunity that all but a few edibles reduce them to an allergic wreck. This condition will be dealt with in Chapter 8.

Monitoring Progress with Bio-energetic Evaluation

Apart from assessment of allergies, bio-energetic instruments can monitor the progress of the patient's return to health and assist the therapist in checking which remedies are suitable during the various stages of recovery, their frequency and size of dosage. Most importantly, the causal chain can be established. The particular organ which is the weakest and which generally constitutes the origin of disease is determined. There may be other organ or tissue problems which flow on from the most stressed organ. Thus we may observe that a sluggish liver causes a congested lymphatic system which finally results in a focus of disease in teeth, sinus or appendix. In such a case it would be useless to treat the tooth or sinus without getting to the cause, which in this case resides in the liver.

'Biological Age' or 'Index'. One of the most challenging concepts pioneered by Schimmel, the founder of Vega testing, is that of the 'biological age' or 'index'. Various

72 FRONTIERS OF NATURAL THERAPIES

homoeopathic dilutions of mesenchyme tissue are matched against the patient by placing test ampoules in the circuit. The tissue is in a graded series corresponding with the health of a very young person and extends through to a 'biological age' which corresponds to the last stages of chronic disease such as malignancy. In a few moments the therapist is therefore able to find the chronicity of the disease pattern and to cross-check this with suitable remedies for the client. During subsequent visits, provided the correct remedies have been chosen and the life-style of the patient has improved, the 'biological age' or 'index' will be found to decrease until normal. It is interesting to observe how this index will fluctuate during times of stress and acute illness.[2]

CASE HISTORIES

June, aged forty-seven, is a good example of the help that Vega evaluation can give in a crisis which in her case looked quite serious indeed. June has been attending intermittently for treatment over several years. Her original history included a tendency to irritable bowel syndrome with possible colitis and hot flushes which developed following a total hysterectomy for hormonal imbalance. When the bowel was affected she had diarrhoea and abdominal pain. During the first months of treatment she had a lot of family worries. The bowel was successfully treated with natural remedies and a year went by before June attended again, this time for a scalp condition involving the skin problem called psoriasis. There was some problem with adhesions from the previous abdominal operation and there had been a further operation for a large benign cyst. These problems were also resolved and another year later June returned to have help for healing her foot which had been involved in a very bad accident with a plate glass door.

During the year before this new crisis (which was before I was using Vega analysis), June had continued on liver and lymphatic cleansing herbs, vitamin C and vitamin E, a zinc compound for the adhesion tendency and specific homoeopathic drops for the psoriasis of the scalp. Then she did not visit the clinic for two and a half months, during which time she had a lot of emotional stress. She developed severe abdominal pain on several occasions with some bleeding from the rectum, symptoms which usually cause everyone to think in terms of bowel blockage. The question was whether she had trouble from the adhesions with associated spasm and blockage or whether there could be a malignancy. Her doctor decided that if there were any more bouts of the pain and bleeding, exploratory surgery would have to be undertaken.

June's iris is interesting in that she has both indication for spasm, as seen by multiple cramp rings around the fairly fine structure of her brown iris, and also the toxic bowel pockets which show up as radial lines moving out from the edge of the pupil throughout the gastrointestinal tract. I had been using the Vega for about three months at the time of her next visit and was concerned to find that her 'biological age' or 'index' (see above) was into the possible malignant range and that the bowel showed up as the most affected organ.

She was given magnesium orotate for bowel spasm, and three complexes of homoeopathic drops; for the bowel mucosa, for the lymphatic drainage and for the liver. Her vitamin C and E were continued. As she lived a fair distance from the clinic she was given two months' treatment and told to report immediately if there were any more problems of pain and bleeding. The medical doctor was also involved with regular visits.

On her return visit in two months, June reported complete freedom from the previous symptoms and the 'biological index' of the bowel had reduced to within the clinical range as distinct from the pathological range of two months before. The scar tissue was still showing up as a problem and also the gall bladder. The treatment was repeated with the addition of homoeopathic magnesium phosphate in the 200th potency for any remaining spasm from the scar tissue. Two months later she was in excellent health with all organs registering a normal reading by the Vega evaluation and a 'biological age' within normal limits. She continued treatment for some months before tapering off to one dose daily, just enough to keep the psoriasis problem on her scalp resolved. The 'biological age' remained stabilised in the healthy range.

Win, aged sixty-six, is a good example of the advantage of monitoring a serious condition through Vega analysis. She had a serious kidney condition which was severe enough in terms of kidney failure to warrant kidney dialysis treatment. At one stage this was undertaken several times per week for a period of several months. When I first met Win she had undergone four months of naturopathic treatment and was currently irrigating her own kidneys through a bag attached to the abdomen, using a sterile solution four times daily. Problems had arisen with continual infections caused by using this method of irrigation.

By Vega analysis, the kidney had a 'biological age' of fourteen on her first visit to me and this is well into the range of pathology. The specialist had said she would have to go back onto hospital dialysis. Win's iris indicated a good inherited constitution and her nephritic syndrome appeared to have resulted from over-indulgence in analgesics earlier in her life. The secondary factor which showed up in her Vega analysis was a congested lymphatic system and, being closely related to immunity, this factor was the cause of the recurrent infection.

The basic minerals of calcium phosphate and potassium sulphate were continued, as were garlic capsules and vitamin C for cleansing and for promoting immunity. Special homoeopathic drops were prepared to remove the specific toxins associated with the nephritis and hopefully to reverse the destructive process. Other homoeopathic drops for toning kidney action were also dispensed. On her second visit, the 'biological age' of the kidney had moved out of the pathological range. Win had been advised by the specialist that dialysis was not needed at the moment. The same treatment was continued with the addition of a large herbal mixture of Violet Leaves, Red Clover, Burdock, Echinacea and Dandelion to control the recurrent infections which had again become a problem.

On the third visit the 'biological age' of the kidney was reduced to within the normal range and no infections had occurred during the month. Win is now reducing the number of times she irrigates the kidneys and is feeling in very good health, which has been stabilised for several months. In a case like this where a pathological process is involved, monitoring of the 'biological age' is very valuable to assess treatment.

Earth Energies and Geopathic Stress

Another very significant area pioneered by Schimmel in terms of diagnosis is geopathic stress. I was first introduced to earth energies in terms of their positive and negative effects, through another pioneer of life energies—Frances Nixon. Nixon found that there is a two-way connecting link between the energy field of an individual and the energy field of the earth. This connection was found to be established during the two-month period before birth and was named the Vivaxis (axis of life) by Nixon. She developed techniques which allowed a person to improve health and energies by aligning themselves with the exact direction of the Vivaxis. The distance from the location to the present place of abode is not relevant. Disturbances in health and all stages of disease were found by Nixon to correspond to a degree of interference with the Vivaxis channel.[3]

Many factors were found to block the energy flow and these included electromagnetic interference from power lines and electric machines, X-rays, scans, radiation from natural sources such as rocks, electrical treatments of various kinds as, for example, diathermy, drugs, insecticides, and many chemicals found in the environment. Medical scientists such as Becker have noted the very small changes in magnetic fields which can have a direct bearing on growth and development. It is quite likely that in the near future, any type of electrical technology will be closely scrutinised to assess the radiation effect on living tissues.

Further research by Nixon resulted in the finding of energy layers every 3 to 3·6 metres in a vertical direction. These layers appear to carry harmonics of all the energies necessary for life, and also include destructive man-made frequencies such as insecticides and other forms of radiation. Nixon developed further techniques to train individuals to tune into the positive frequencies of life-giving elements such as oxygen, magnesium, calcium and selenium. Other techniques aid the removal of frequencies related to heavy metals such as cadmium, lead and mercury. Techniques include the treating of food to remove the effect of pesticide residues and the removal of static from clothes and articles of furniture.

Nixon was very interested in the work of medical scientists like Becker, as she found that the means of focusing and identifying the various positive and harmful elements was related to magnetic crystals near the pineal gland. By means of this focusing mechanism, individuals were trained to identify underground energy flows which have a detrimental effect on the health and also to monitor the extent of electromagnetic fields from power lines and various electrical installations as, for example, microwave antennae.

A number of physicists became interested in the work of Nixon and studied with her at her home on Thetis Island, Vancouver. Many thousands of persons were trained by Nixon, including a team of instructors. The techniques are unique in that they require no technological aids and no assistance from a therapist. An individual learns to monitor their own health, negative and positive energies in the environment and to use beneficial earth energies to reinstate balance and health. Although the work of Nixon is unique in identifying geopathic stress with our own faculties, the area has been explored over the last few decades within a variety of disciplines.

Geopathic stress is the term used for the detrimental effect of a number of adverse geological energies or influences. In former times this whole area was restricted to the interest of dowsers and a few enlightened architects. In parts of Europe, particularly in West Germany, geopathic stress now has a measure of respectability, especially in relation to a growing group of engineers and architects. A number of studies have correlated cancer development with persons situated in a particular location within a house.[4] These locations especially concern underground waterstreams and their interaction with energy grids known as Curry and Hartman grids, so named after their discoverers. If a bed happens to be located over an intersection of several negative influences then the possibility for cancer development is greatly increased. It appears that the electromagnetic field is detrimentally altered in such positions.

The effect may be made more lethal depending on the electrical circuitry of the home and may involve the proximity of high-tension power lines.

The Curry and Hartman grids are two grids based on intersecting lines only a metre or so apart. It would therefore be impossible to avoid placing all furniture in a house outside their sphere of influence. The important consideration is to avoid the intersections of the grids and their interaction with other factors. Thus there may be an area of only half a metre in circumference which is very detrimental to health and which can easily be avoided if one is able to locate the critical points. There are now several instruments developed which help to find these critical positions in a house but they all require some dowsing ability. (Dowsing ability is the ability to develop a degree of clairsentience and this is also called the radiesthesia sense. About 90 per cent of people are able to develop some ability in this direction with practice.[5])

It might seem a very time-consuming and expensive business to make these evaluations of geopathic stress on a property or individual. However, Schimmel has itemised substances which can be used in a test kit in conjunction with the Vega instrument. There is a test for electromagnetic stress, for radiation, one for the Hartman and another for the Curry Grid, others for oil and underground streams and so on. The therapist still needs the sensitivity to test the individuals for these conditions, but it is much easier for a therapist to be able to undertake such evaluations in the consulting room by using Vegatesting. Techniques have also been devised to locate the particular part of the body which is affected so that the relevant section of the bed is pin-pointed and the bed relocated without the therapist needing to visit the house.

_____ CASE HISTORY _____

A typical case in my practice concerned Andrew, aged sixteen. His continual exhaustion was beginning to undermine studies at school. A common symptom of geopathic stress manifested in this case involving great exhaustion upon waking and relief when sleeping away from home. A course of the usual minerals and herbs and Bach flowers for nervous exhaustion had no effect on Andrew. After two months of treatment I tested him by Vega diagnosis for geopathic stress. There was a positive reading for the Hartman grid so he was advised to move the bed about 1 metre. After initial protests by his mother, who was concerned about the small size of the bedroom, this rearrangement was made.

On the next visit I observed a complete change to Andrew's face — his colour had improved and there was more indication of 'aliveness' about his features. These observations were underscored by his report of improved energy and more refreshing sleep. His 'biological age' which was previously fixed too high for a sixteen year-old reduced to a normal level. His condition was monitored for several months and there was no relapse.

It should be mentioned that therapists have discovered that detoxification of the patient along standard naturopathic lines with herbs and homoeopathics is unable to take place while the patient is subject to geopathic stress. Furthermore, the patient often has pronounced aggravations from homoeopathic treatment when this problem is not addressed. Many therapy-resistant patients are found to fall into this category. Underground oil and water streams, and the Curry and Hartman grids are naturally occurring phenomena, but in many cultures we find evidence that there is awareness of the need to locate houses away from certain areas. With the addition of all the man-made electrical sources of interference, geopathic stress is becoming a concern of some significance to therapists who understand the phenomenon.

It could be said then that with bio-energetic testing technology has now come to the aid of the natural therapist. Evaluation of important criteria such as the level and balance of energy in the body, the underlying causes of disease patterns, identification of allergens, selection of remedies which match the patient's own energy pattern, and the monitoring of progress back towards health may all be established easily and relatively cheaply. Much of the guesswork is being taken out of diagnosis and prescribing, although a subjective factor is recognised. Further research is under way to indicate that consistent results can be obtained between therapists, and also to develop new instruments which are less dependent on any subjective or variable factor.

CHAPTER 7

Toxaemia – The Twentieth-Century Plague

What do naturopaths mean when they talk about a body full of toxins? Where do these toxins come from and how do we get rid of them? Are allergies related to toxins? What part does heredity play in toxaemia? How does the accumulation of toxins relate to lowered vitality? Why does becoming healthy involve a healing crisis? How do we know whether we are having a healing or disease crisis?

Toxaemia and Nineteenth-Century Naturopathic Medicine

The twin concepts of building up vitality or energy and resolving and eliminating toxins are basic to all natural medicine. These ideas were promoted by the early naturopaths in Germany nearly two hundred years ago. We find a vastly different environment today from Europe in the nineteenth century. In those days the toxins which accumulated in the body did not result from junk food or chemical environmental pollution or from modern drugs. Poor diet may have resulted from an overload of meat in the case of the wealthy, or insufficient fresh fruit and vegetables in the case of the poor. Refined flour, grains and sugar were unknown, water was uncontaminated with chemicals from factory effluent, and air did not contain the types of chemical pollution experienced now.[1]

It is true that certain classes of workers, such as coal miners or chimney sweeps, suffered problems from environmental toxins. Whole classes of persons would have been too poor to buy fresh fruit and vegetables and certainly such produce would not have been available all the year round as it is today. There was air pollution in certain areas from the burning of coal but it can hardly compare with the situation in a number of major cities today. The following list includes only some of the ever-growing toxic problems which governments are belatedly addressing in the latter part of this century.

POLLUTANTS IN THE TWENTIETH CENTURY

- **Food additives** including colourings, flavourings, preservatives, bleaches, emulsifiers, and stabilisors.

- **Air pollution** from fluorocarbons, nitric acid, sulphuric acid, and lead in the atmosphere.

- **Water pollution** from nitrates, chlorine, hydrofluoric acid, lime and insecticides.

- **Earth pollution** from heavy metals used in industry and farming such as mercury and from superphosphates and insecticides.

- **Electromagnetic pollution** from high-tension overhead wires and from many technological developments used in industry and the home.

We should also contrast the situation of the past century with that of our era in terms of infectious disease. Before the age of antibiotics, infections were a major cause of high levels of infant mortality and also a cause of premature death in older persons. The role of infection and inflammation as a response to toxaemia therefore forms another important theme in this discussion. The natural therapist understands fever and inflammation in a totally different way from orthodox medicine. One of the typical responses by individuals to the increasing toxic overload of our century is to manifest a wide range of inflammatory disorders which now go by the name of allergies.

Allergies — the Modern Trend

One result of the many chemicals to which we subject our bodies is the development of that modern catch-phrase — an allergy. Allergies are found to take many forms. Basically the unpleasant symptoms associated with allergies are the reaction by the body to a substance which it recognises as foreign but with which it is not able to resolve or remove. The recognition of the allergy by the immune system constitutes reactions which include running eyes and nose, diarrhoea, abdominal pain, constipation, headaches, hayfever, asthma, insomnia, irritability, dermatitis, and exhaustion.[2] How could one avoid exhaustion in the face of such discomfort! Many of the symptoms listed result from inflammation following the release of histamine from the mast cells in the blood. Histamine causes swelling and inflammation of the skin and mucous membranes. The usual medical response is to give an antihistamine or cortisone in various forms. Both these medications suppress inflammation but do not treat the cause of the allergy. Histamine will be discussed later in terms of its particular role in the inflammatory response and its negative effect when inflammation is suppressed by drugs.

Allergies and Diet. The natural therapist is dedicated to treating the whole person. There can be more to allergies than removing the affecting substances. It has been pointed out in the previous chapter that some people may be shown to have so many food allergies that their social life becomes a nightmare or nonexistent. We should certainly endeavour to have food and water in as natural a state as possible. The basic diet advocated in my clinic emphasises a diet largely concentrating on wholegrain cereals, seeds and fresh nuts (especially almonds), salads and steamed vegetables, a moderate amount of soft cheese provided dairy allergies are not too prominent, a selection of ripe fruit, and small helpings only of meat, fish or poultry if eaten. The diet sheet includes a list of foods to exclude as, until recently, people did not understand what was in junk food. A sample diet is suggested.

This sheet has been used by many clinics and groups and needed little amplification throughout the 1970s and into the beginning of the 1980s. Then suddenly, more and more clients had problems even with the simplest articles of food. Yeast was a typical example and had to be removed from the diet sheet as a healthy additive which everyone should add to their orange juice. Monilia or thrush (*Candida albicans*) developed almost in plague proportions and thus all food with yeast had to be removed from the diet. Dried fruit also went off the list of good foods—people with thrush were instantly worsened by the inclusion of concentrated amounts of even natural sugars. Hypoglycaemia was another accompanying plague which overflowed the waiting rooms of natural therapists and nutritionally-inclined doctors.

_____ CASE HISTORIES _____

Damien, aged seventeen, was the most severe migraine case I have ever treated. He came to the clinic after three years of hemiplegic migraines. The attacks began with tingling in hands, headache, and vomiting which was so severe that the blood vessels in the stomach became ruptured. During attacks he became totally paralysed down one side. He had suffered no less than six of these attacks between short intervals, before his first visit. Duration of the attacks was 12 to 15 hours. The iris revealed a good basic constitution and there was one strong acute nerve ring in the iris. The 'biological age' was raised, with the liver showing as the most stressed organ, followed by the lymphatic system. There were allergies to dairy produce and peanut butter. The diet was not particularly good—no breakfast; vegetables and meat at his place of work at midday; and frequently, junk food at night.

His first month of treatment included homoeopathic liver and lymph drops, plus a herbal extract tablet for the liver. A homoeopathic antidote was made for the food allergies and other toxic substances affecting the lymphatic system. The minerals magnesium, potassium and calcium phosphate were given for the central nervous system plus vitamin B-complex and vitamin C for general detoxification.

Improvement surpassed all expectations. Damien did not have a single headache during the six months of treatment. Over this time he improved his diet and the treatment was then tapered off with no relapse. Having rebalanced his organs and with improved physiological function, he was able to have small amounts of dairy produce without creating a problem.

Helen, aged thirty-six, attended with pain and discomfort in the stomach after eating bread, biscuits, cake, and fats. This is a suitable case to give as an example because the iris illustrated an accumulation of waste in the body moving outwards from the gastrointestinal tract. This had then burdened the lymphatic stystem which showed up through the iris in the typical pattern of white/brown clouds. (See section on iris diagnosis later in this chapter.) Another interesting finding in Helen's iris was the presence of the inherited markers called psoric spots. These look like brown freckles through the iris and indicate an inherited tendency for allergic, inflammatory reaction. In spite of her fairly healthy diet the stage was thus set for problems and it took very little environmental stress to set off these problems.

Helen came to the clinic feeling tired and sluggish and also reported a history of genital Herpes when under stress. She has a good attitude towards life and is outgoing and cheerful. Vega analysis indicated that she had allergies to yeast, Vegemite (which contains yeast), wheat and oats. The stomach was indicated as the most stressed organ and as Helen was overweight it was of interest that the thyroid showed as sluggish. It was explained that although it would be necessary to keep off the allergy-producing foods at the moment, later, when a degree of detoxification had taken place and the digestive organs toned, these articles of food would probably no longer be a problem. This approach is probably the main difference in the handling of allergies by natural therapists and that of the orthodox profession which usually restricts the offending substances for ever.

Treatment for Helen during the first month included a herbal digestive mixture containing Marshmallow, Melissa, Angelica, Dandelion, Burdock and Centaury, homoeopathically prepared sodium phosphate after meals, kelp and homoeopathic drops for the thyroid, and two further homoeopathic preparations to antidote toxins in the system and tone digestive organs. All the remedies enhance elimination of waste. Nothing was given directly for energy, but on her return visit Helen reported feeling fantastic with lots of energy. This underscores the devitalising and exhausting effect of a system loaded with toxins. The prescription was repeated for a second month with the addition of homoeopathic Natrum Muriaticum in the 200th potency for the Herpes tendency.

Helen continued to improve and will soon be tapering off treatment, although she may have to keep off wheat and yeast for some time yet. As with many people, these foods only act as allergies in the presence of many toxins and particular weaknesses of digestive capacity. In the case of Helen, the stomach no longer shows up as a stressed organ via Vega analysis, and the iris, which indicates changes very slowly, is gradually changing colour. When the cleansing process is complete, she may be able to tolerate wheat and yeast in moderate amounts.

The most logical explanation for the increase of allergies rests with the enormous strain placed on the average immune system by the thousands of foreign chemicals which are present in our food, air and water. Perhaps the most telling figures relate to the increase of deaths from asthma in the last few years. Asthma is a condition involving a dangerous increase in sticky mucus in the bronchial tree plus a degree of swelling and spasm in the breathing passages. Many asthmatics are worsened by breathing polluted air or by eating certain foods. Asthma problems can be used as a measuring stick for the increase of severe allergies in our community.

It is impractical to remove more and more foodstuffs from the diet when we know that the main problem is the inability of the body to cope with the ever increasing load of chemicals. For instance, a diet largely consisting of fresh fruit and vegetables still contains pesticide residues. There is still scientific controversy about the acceptable levels of these pesticides, and chemicals which were once thought to be safe are now banned from agricultural use. What should we do to deal with the toxaemia which leads to allergies?

Infections and Toxaemia

The manifestation of allergies is certainly not the only evidence of toxins in the body. Now that antibiotics and steroids are available we have tended to forget the risks and emphasis formerly placed on infections as a major cause of death and disease. Statistics record the reduction of deaths and serious illness from infections which has taken place since penicillin, sulphonamides and steroids were introduced earlier this century. Thinking people wonder if there is any connection between the diminishment of infectious disease and the great increase of chronic disease which has taken place in the second half of this century.[3]

One of the interesting differences between the orthodox approach to infections and that of natural therapists is the role attached by natural therapists to bacteria and viruses in the disease cycle. Bacteria are understood by natural therapists as having an important role to play in the release of toxins. They are part of the chain involved in inflammatory disease and the degree of their presence is understood as directly related to the amount of toxins present in the system. Since last century it has been the view of naturopaths that bacteria are attracted to a toxic body as flies would be to a rubbish tip. Once the rubbish in the form of toxins is resolved through fever and inflammation which is handled correctly, the bacteria automatically disappear.

In the management of inflammation we have therefore, two diametrically opposed views. A child presenting with tonsillitis will be given a totally different treatment by an orthodox doctor and a natural therapist. The natural therapist looks at the tonsils as the gateway to the lymphatic system and infected tonsils are understood as a sign that the lymphatic system needs urgent cleansing. The diet of the child will be examined to see if he or she is eating too many refined foods which would overload the body with toxins. Significant reduction of dairy produce will be suggested and these would be replaced with fruit juice. Cleansing herbs like Phytolacca, Burdock, Violet Leaves and Red Clover will be administered. Vitamin C and the tissue salts Ferrum Phosphate and Kali Muriaticum are given to stimulate the immune system and resolve toxins. Specific homoeopathic remedies which may be used are Belladonna for fever, and Hepar Sulphuricus or Mercurius Biniodatum for pus formation.

The natural treatment does not suppress the inflammation but keeps it from developing into any life threatening situation. The fever is kept within certain limits but not suppressed; the immune system is stimulated, and the health of vital and eliminative organs enhanced so that toxins may be excreted as quickly as possible. The final outcome is experienced to be decreasing attacks of tonsillitis as toxins are eliminated and health and immunity improved.

The orthodox medical approach is to give antibiotics at the first sign of infected tonsils. These drugs are quite often administered before infection develops simply because the tonsils are enlarged, in which case the drugs achieve nothing! The body not only has the inflammatory process forestalled but must also cope with the detoxifying of the drug and this places an additional burden on the liver and kidneys.

There are a number of structures in the body which deal with elimination of toxins. First, there is the liver which is like a major metabolic factory dealing with all drugs and chemicals. It detoxifies foreign substances by breaking them down into simple substances which can be excreted by the organs of elimination. These organs are the bowel, kidneys, lungs and skin. Poor or sluggish functioning in any of these organs will result in retention of toxic waste and possible overload to the system.

Even in the case of normal unadulterated food, the digestive organs have the task of 'denaturing' the food so that it is no longer a 'foreign' substance and can be assimilated for growth and energy. A sluggishness in any of the digestive organs can thus result in accumulation of toxins from even a healthy diet. It is easy to see how toxins can accelerate in a tired and stressed body even apart from the overload of chemicals in our present environment. Here, we can relate diminished vitality to accumulation of toxins and conversely, the elimination of toxins can follow improvement of energy.

Secondly, the lymphatic or reticulendothelial system is involved with antigen/antibody formation and with the production of white blood cells which play an important part in infections, toxic conditions and ingestion of foreign or unwanted particles. The liver is also responsible for the production of antibodies. The nervous system is involved with reflex excitation and irritation responses and recently, considerable research has indicated the influence that the nervous system can have on immunity.[4] The endocrine system, in particular the adrenal and pituitary glands, also plays a part in the inflammatory process.

Therefore, the whole health of the body is involved in immunity and if any part is lacking in tone and precision the body becomes liable to disease. The holistic approach of natural medicine is very suited to balancing and regulating the body so that all these systems can play their correct roles. A natural flow then takes place and toxins released from foods and various environmental factors are eliminated adequately through the normal channels of elimination. In the case of imbalance in these various systems of defence, excretion of toxins into the tissues takes place and inflammation ensues. Disease may follow and takes place in various stages. Before discussing these stages it is appropriate to briefly discuss iridology in terms of the toxic factor.

Iridology and Toxaemia

In many patients we find through iris diagnosis that the lymphatic system has been congested for many years and this has predisposed the person to allergies from the basic overload of toxins in the system. These are the persons who often develop eczema and asthma from an early age. They start with an accumulation of toxins perhaps commencing *in utero*, and then, with a poor diet and environmental pollution, they soon succumb to a multitude of allergies. A congested lymphatic system is indicated in the iris by clouds of white-brown markings just inside the edge of the iris. Sometimes a person with a good life-style may exhibit these markings without any particular health problem. It is a sign of weakness in the immune system and as such is valuable to the therapist.

It has been mentioned that disease often starts in the gastrointestinal tract and the area in the iris immediately around the pupil corresponds to this part of the anatomy and physiology. Toxins here show as clouds of white matter (intestinal and gastric fermentation), brown discolourations (accumulation of toxins from incompletely digested food), and black pockets and lines (degenerative processes involving the gastrointestinal tract).

Discolourations can also occur near the edge of the iris in the form of white rings partial or complete (artiosclerosis) and a darkish discolouration around the edge of the iris, called the scurf rim, which indicates toxins below the skin and poor elimination through the skin.[5]

This is a simplified summary. The main fact to remember is that a toxin-free body is illustrated in the iris by the absence of any colour except the clear natural colour which should be the same from the edge of the iris to the pupil. With change of life-style and with natural therapies of various types the colour of the iris gradually improves. Clients often notice the improvement themselves. In cases of heavy toxaemia the process can take several years but the result is permanent.

The role of the natural therapist is to educate the client to a healthy life-style so that environmental toxins are minimised, nutrition improved, relaxation and creativity enhanced and physical therapies prescribed which will augment the defence systems and boost body energies and organ function.

CHAPTER 8

The Stages of Disease

How does the natural therapist see the relationship of acute and chronic disease processes? How would people respond in treatment to the various stages of disease? Why do natural therapists dislike the process of immunisation against acute disease?

Creating balance and harmony at all levels of being is the key to health. Disease is suffered by a person out of balance. In this chapter only physical imbalance will be discussed but it must be remembered that possibly the greatest trigger to physical imbalance is emotional conflict. This will be dealt with in Chapter 12. The stages of disease correspond to the degree of imbalance in the person.

Health involves a free flow of energy to all parts of the body and the stages of disease may be discussed in several ways. The models are based on slightly different viewpoints but each demonstrates a flow or movement between what is taken in from food and the environment. There are considerations as to whether food is adequately broken up, absorbed and excreted, and the stasis and subsequent disease which develops from an interruption to the flowing process. Thus, natural therapists do not see disease as a particular entity which arrives in the body by chance either as an infection or, at the other end of the scale, as a maligant tumour.

The classical model presented by naturopaths for many decades involves the chain of toxins, inflammation and fever

The Three Stages of Disease

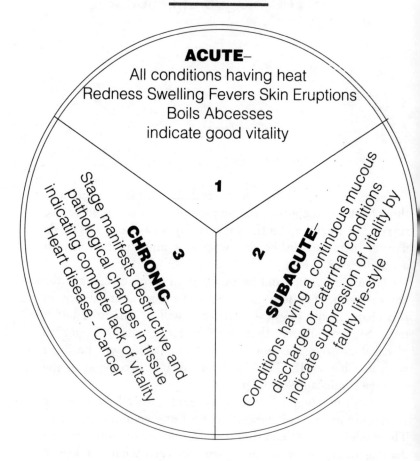

plus resolution of toxins, provided body energies are adequate. In the absence of the energy needed to provide for good immune function, inflammation does not take place, and more chronic sub-acute inflammation takes place. Thus ezcema or fever may progress to asthma and chronic bronchial discharges. Further suppression through poor life-style and drugs results in more serious degenerative disease such as arthritis, sclerosis and, in the extreme case, cancer. With natural treatment, these stages are experienced as reversing back to health and the process is known as retracing.

One could summarise the naturopathic model for the stages of disease in the following way. If a person is born with a good hereditary health pattern and has a healthy life-style with a diet consisting largely of foods in their natural state, there is no reason why they should not live into their eighties without severe acute or chronic disease. A healthy life-style includes right rhythm in the areas of sleep, relaxation, sex and work. In other words, the life is well spaced and the person therefore enjoys both psychological and physical health. In this brief generalisation we are not concerned with those persons who in spite of good health, heredity and life-style, destroy themselves with some extraordinary eccentricity.

The next consideration in our summary is the individual who is born with reasonable health heredity but is mismanaged from birth according to naturopathic practice and philosophy. The chain of ill health may start with a mother keen on having an uninterrupted day at work so that the baby is bottle-fed from the first weeks of life. A formula will never replace the positive effect of the mother's milk containing all the life-sustaining nutriments in just the right quantities plus the enzymes necessary for stimulating the digestion of the baby. These enzymes are not present in formula milk. The same problem may be continued with the use of bottled and tinned food after the baby is weaned. A naturopath sees many diseases as starting with a weak or over-burdened digestion.

The effect of poorly metabolised food from an unnatural diet is that toxins gradually accumulate in the system of the small child. The natural reaction of this developing toxaemia is for the vital body of the child to manifest a fever and this will be concurrent with a particular infection such as one of the common childhood fevers or other systemic inflammations. During the heat or inflammation which ensues, waste in the system is broken down to simpler molecules and excreted via the normal channels of skin, lungs, kidney and bowel. There are many natural approaches using vitamin C, mineral compounds, herbs and homoeopathy to assist this process of inflammation. Provided the fever is not suppressed, the child is given a fresh start and health and vitality are improved.

The result of immunisation on the immune system of the child should be mentioned here. Immunisation is not just a controversial subject between health departments and natural therapists.[1] There is controversy within the medical profession. Thus a professor of preventive medicine was able to show through graphs in a well-publicised book that the incidence of most infectious diseases declined without the help of immunisation programmes.[2] It has been suggested by some medical scientists that the increase of chronic disease processes in childhood, such as leukaemia and cancer, may relate to suppression of acute disease through immunisation programmes. The high incidence of childhood asthma is understood by natural therapists to have the same cause.

There is no question that immunisation prevents the spread of certain infections, but what is the cost to the healthy functioning of the immune system? There are a number of ways to control and manage the diseases for which immunisation is usually administered. There are also ways to protect the pregnant woman from Rubella and other viruses which may produce congenital abnormalities. Adequate quantities of vitamin C during pregnancy will protect the foetus against any virus and poor immunity can be aided by zinc compounds, particular herbs and homoeopathic remedies. There are also specific homoeopathic remedies for most infectious diseases.

The Acute Stage of Disease

Manifestation of infectious fever or inflammation such as in tonsillitis is called the acute stage of disease. It is characterised by heat, redness, skin rashes and eruptions. In the older person it may also be characterised by any skin eruption such as eczema, dermatitis and acne or by other inflammatory conditions. Gout is another typical example of an acute metabolic

The Circle of Disease

Negative emotions
Lack of rest – sunlight – exercise
gives exhaustion of all cells

ENERVATION – NERVOUS EXHAUSTION

TOXAEMIA – INTERNAL POLLUTION

Refined foods
Dyes – Preservatives – Flavourings
Water and Air Pollution – Insecticides
Artificial Fertilisers

disorder which manifests as a painfully acute swelling of the large toe and surrounding area and is characterised by heat, redness and swelling.

_____CASE HISTORIES_____

Tony, aged thirty-nine, had suffered gout intermittently for two years and arrived at the clinic on crutches. His work involved tiling floors so gout was a considerable inconvenience. Gout is an acute reaction to an accumulation of toxic waste, usually as a result of dietary indiscretions which create an acid milieu in the tissues. This fact was partly confirmed by an analysis of Tony's diet which consisted of eggs, white bread, fried chicken, take-away lunches and lots of roasts at night. There was little emphasis on fruit and salad. Typically for gout, the liver showed up with Vega diagnosis as the most stressed organ with a raised 'biological age' which was at a clinically significant, but not pathological stage.

In the first month of treatment Tony was given sodium phosphate in specially prepared form to alkalinise the tissues, herbal liver and rheumatic compounds, a mineral combination for the inflammation, vitamins B6 and C. On his return visit after one month he reported feeling better after two weeks and the 'biological age' of the liver was found to be reduced to within normal range. In all, Tony had four months' treatment and during this time changed his diet. There was no return of the problem.

_____

There are some acute cases where orthodox medicine cannot help at all and Edward was such an instance. At the age of thirty-one, he developed severe iritis and came to visit me after six weeks of pain in the eye and with no relief fom the standard treatment of cortisone and atropine. As an indication of the build-up of acid in the tissues and the predisposition to acute inflammation, he had also suffered from gout. His diet was a classic example for the development of such a situation. It consisted of white bread, jam, cheese, steak, chips, fish fingers plus some salad and vegetables. The iris revealed moderate lymphatic congestion and the 'biological age' was raised according to Vegatesting, with the liver again showing as the most stressed organ. This was in keeping with the diet.

The first month of treatment included specially prepared sodium phosphate for the acidity in the tissues, zinc for healing and to prevent scarring, herbal and homoeopathic liver remedies, specific drops for the eye containing homoeopathic remedies Euphrasia, Hypericum, and Mercurius Corrosivus, iron phosphate for the inflammatory process in the eye and a specially prepared homoeopathic antidote for particular toxins as evaluated by Vegatesting.

In two weeks Edward returned with the report that all pain in the eye had ceased and vision had improved. He was off the cortisone and had changed his diet. The 'biological age' was now fairly normal. The treatment was continued for another two weeks and there was no relapse with the eye problem. He was sent away with a second month of treatment to consolidate his rebalanced biochemistry.

The Sub-acute Stage of Disease

If fever is suppressed by antibiotics, salycilates (aspirin) or steroids (cortisone), the toxins sink deeper into the system and set up a sub-acute inflammation. In the child this often manifests as bronchial asthma, recurrent colds, or ear infections. In the adult recurrent colds and flu plus chronic sinusitis may manifest. Many adults are also prone to asthma attacks. The experience of sub-clinical states such as a constant feeling of unwellness and tiredness with slight aching in different parts of the body is typical of the sub-acute stage of disease. Allergies also feature prominently in this stage. Thus, a particular food or foreign protein will often trigger off flu-like symptoms of vague unwellness. The sub-acute stage is characterised by chronic inflammation of a low-grade type accompanied by mucous discharge from any site.[3]

The usual treatment for this stage is further drugs which may include antihistamines for inflamed mucous membranes, broncho-dilators for asthma, and cortisone for most stubborn cases. Unfortunately, the inflammatory process is further suppressed, often completely, and chronic disease may then manifest. This final stage of the disease process is characterised by destruction of tissue as occurs in arthritis, multiple sclerosis, nephritis, cardio-vascular disease, bronchial diseases, and finally our arch enemy—cancer.

It is very rewarding to be able to break this chain of disease in a child and know that they will then progress towards health from that point of time.

_____ CASE HISTORY _____

Andrew was a typical case of childhood asthma which commenced when he was eighteen months old. At the time of commencing treatment he was on the asthma 'pump' and oral medication, and had recently been hospitalised for a bad attack. His attacks usually started with a running nose, underlining the characteristics of the sub-acute stage previously described. There were no other family members with asthma.

Andrew's brown iris presented quite a good fine structure with some nerve rings. As in the previous two cases, by Vega diagnosis the liver again showed up as the most stressed organ indicating (as in many asthma cases), an underlying digestive problem with possible allergies. The bronchial system showed up as a secondary problem to the liver, and the last significant factor in this particular causal chain was indicated by Vega analysis as the sinuses.

The first month of treatment included calcium phosphate tablets as the basic tissue salt needed for Andrew's constitution; the mineral combination of iron phosphate and potassium chloride in specially prepared form for the inflammation and mucus of bronchial passages; vitamin C for immunity and mucus resolution; homoeopathic liver and lymphatic cleansing drops and lastly, a herbal tincture of Ammi Visnagi and Thyme for broncho-dilating purposes.

On his return visit the liver was found to have reduced in 'biological age' to normal and there had been no further asthma attacks. The treatment was continued and during the second month there was one bad attack following a cold. The treatment was continued with the addition of homoeopathic drops to antidote any inherited tubercular taint in the family, often the basis for asthma (see Chapter 11). Additional homoeopathic drops were added to remove any side-effects of immunisation and toxins from past food allergies.

During the fifth month of treatment Andrew had a cold without an asthma attack and this was a definite milestone. The following month he had one very bad attack which commenced with a cough. The homoeopathic remedies were changed to cope more adequately with his severe allergies to animal fur. Although he had the two bad attacks mentioned during the first few months of treatment, recovery from each was much quicker than usual and he is off medical drugs between these now infrequent attacks. The 'biological age' via Vega diagnosis is stabilised in the normal range.

The Retracing Phenomenon

During naturopathic treatment the patient will go backwards through the various stages of illness. For instance, an arthritic patient may develop recurrent colds, and then finally, if a perfect example, a skin rash. The education of the client as to what to expect during the course of treatment is therefore essential.

During a crisis involving the re-establishment of the inflammatory process, the patient may feel very ill and toxic. If there has been no understanding of the healing process, the first thing the family will do is to call the doctor who will immediately repress this important inflammatory stage with drugs. It is this critical inflammatory stage which is called the healing crisis and it results from the body vitality or energy increasing with the aid of natural medicines.

When handled wisely, the healing crisis is never dangerous; the fever is controlled but not suppressed, and the organs of elimination are stimulated to excrete toxins adequately. In the case of young children and in adults of all ages, after a correctly handled acute phase they experience more energy and a greater immunity to infections. The role of bacteria will be seen as a vital part of the inflammatory process and the scientific rationale for this position will be examined in the next chapter.

We can thus see that we have a circle of health and disease. Lowered energy or vitality encourages the accumulation of toxins, which in turn makes us feel more exhausted. It is the role of the therapist to intervene on both sides of the circle and give therapies which both enhance vitality and strengthen organs which are involved with digestion and elimination. Digestive and liver herbs will be given almost universally for toxic conditions. It will have been observed that in several of the case histories the liver showed by Vega analysis as the most stressed organ. The lymphatic system needs to be mentioned here as it is intimately related to the immune system and becomes very clogged when the liver is sluggish over a long period of time.

_____CASE HISTORY_____

The case of Mary, aged forty, is a good illustration of toxaemia moving towards a pathology which may have been reversed just in time. This case also illustrates the value of the several forms of assessment which can be used in synthesis to give a full understanding of the parameters of the case. The personal history indicated that Mary had suffered a lot of stress, had premenstrual headaches, a history of asthma and eczema, Herpes involving the face and left eye, and was currently suffering from swollen glands. Her present diet was good although she was consuming far too much carrot juice and this made it difficult to tell her real colour as the skin had taken on a yellow hue.

Thus, the history of eczema, asthma and swollen glands gave the information of the toxic aspect of her medical condition. This conclusion was confirmed by iris diagnosis as there was a very open structure indicating poor vitality, toxins in the gastrointestinal tract, and heavy lymphatic congestion. The autonomic nervous system indicated considerable imbalance and this is involved with

The Healing Crisis

VITALITY + TOXINS → INFLAMMATION

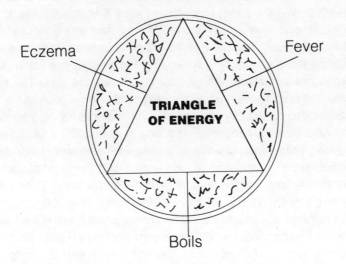

Eczema

Fever

TRIANGLE OF ENERGY

Boils

The Disease Crisis

POOR VITALITY + TOXINS = CHRONIC DISEASE + DEATH

the digestion and endocrine glands. Weakness in the organs of liver, kidneys and bronchials was apparent.

The main problem of concern involved a tumour in the area of the thyroid gland. Some further differential diagnosis was therefore needed. Was the tumour malignant? Was it an expression of the general toxic level in the system? Vegatesting was able to clarify these questions. Yes, the toxins were quite severe and there was a premalignant condition not involving the thyroid, but rather that organ often involved with general toxaemia—the liver. The lymphatic system showed up as the next point of toxic overload in the causal chain of Mary's problem. The first month of treatment involved liver and lymphatic cleansing homoeopathics, including a specific preparation to antidote previous toxins accumulated from poor digestion, allergies and old vaccinations. For general energy, potassium and magnesium phosphate and vitamin B-complex were given. On her first return visit, Mary was feeling better and had not suffered any headaches. The premalignant reading via Vega-testing had disappeared and the organs were now registering in the normal range. The treatment was continued with a change of homoeopathic remedies to work more specifically on the endo-crines and throat area.

After the second month of treatment, the tumour near the thyroid had almost disappeared and Mary was continuing to feel well. Treatment was continued for several more months to continue elimination of toxins and to consolidate the new-found health and well-being. There were no further problems and the growth entirely disappeared. As soon as the detoxification programme was started the tumour had started to diminish.

Confusion can arise when attempts are made to express these theories in acceptable medical or scientific language. Although the experience of 150 years in clinical practice has given the anecdotal and clinical evidence necessary to prove the naturopathic approach, medical and governmental authorities do not always support this approach. More recently, physiological and biochemical research has validated the naturo-pathic principles of handling toxaemia and inflammation.

CHAPTER 9

Toxaemia, Inflammation, Bacteria and Science

How could inflammation and fever be explained in scientific language as a move towards healing and health? Is there a rational reason for bacteria to be in the body without having been 'caught' from an infected person or source? How does fever or inflammation control toxins in the body?

The scientific understanding of naturopathic philosophy has been outlined by the German homoeopath and medical scientist, Dr Hans-Heinrich Reckeweg. Reckeweg has a thorough background in science to serve as a basis for his model of health and disease. He is a graduate in medicine following studies at universities of Wurzburg, Berlin, Münster and Bonn. He also studied pharmacology and toxicology at Bonn University. Later, he studied homoeopathy in Berlin and conducted a homoeopathic practice for nearly thirty years before turning to research and writing. It is significant that this more scientific description of the naturopathic approach comes from Germany where the naturopathic movement started.

Disease processes are seen in three main stages. The first stage involves excretion of toxins into the tissues rather than through the normal channels of elimination. Inflammation results as a response to toxins in the tissues. The next stage involves the depositing of toxins in tissues and this later leads to impregnation of the tissues by toxins. The final stage is degeneration of tissues through the action of toxins, leading to the neoplastic or cancerous process. This is really an exact expression of the traditional naturopathic understanding which Reckeweg accompanies with modern biochemical knowledge.

Reckeweg sees the above disease stages in two broad categories. The first or humoral phase includes excretion, reaction or inflammation, and deposition, and the tendency towards healing is retained by the organism. The enzymes remain intact and the excretion process dominates. The second or cellular phase expresses more deep-seated constitutional disease and involves the impregnation phase, degenerative phases and neoplastic development. The health of the enzymes is the key to the whole subject and their suppression or death through administration of drugs during the inflammatory stage is the main problem.

Reckeweg uses the term homotoxins to describe toxins in the body which derive from various sources. Inflammation is described as a biologically goal-oriented attempt towards detoxification and hence healing. The process of inflammation and detoxification of tissues is briefly described:

> In the past hundred years, the pathogenetic role of bacteria
> has obviously been exaggerated. Bacteria have to fulfill
> an important biological duty. They secrete the enzyme
> hyaluronidase which dissolves connective tissue. Homotoxins
> stored in the connective tissue are set free. The homotoxins, not
> the bacteria are the decisive factor in inflammation. They must
> be detoxified and should, to a certain extent be burned in the
> fire of the reaction phase. Many homotoxins such as false
> proteins, allergy histamine, viruses etc. are burned during the
> inflammation.[1]

If the normal process of detoxification is blocked or suppressed, homotoxins become active in the deep tissues of the body. Chemotherapy with penicillin and sulphonimides causes toxins to go into deeper and deeper structures. Reckeweg sees every allergy as resulting from suppression of the excretion and reaction phases. This reaction or inflammation process is explained as coinciding with acidosis and exists in close connection with the antigen/antibody reaction and not in response to bacteria. The acid reaction can be observed following the puncturing of the skin with an electrode whereby the pH or acidity of the tissue can be measured. The antigen/antibody reaction liberates chemical components such as histamine and the Menkin factor which both initiate inflammation.

Connective tissue is the real theatre of war between the defence systems and toxins. The inflammation and subsequent bacterial invasion release the toxins from the connective tissue so that they can be digested by enzyme activity. It should be mentioned that viruses are understood to be in a quite different category from bacteria in the inflammatory process. Viruses are classed as toxic factors and one of the reasons for not suppressing fever is that a rise in the body of only a few degrees of temperature will kill viruses.[2]

Allergy results from the formation of 'wild' peptides or proteins which are formed when the acid or inflammation stage is interrupted. Homotoxins, unused histamine, bacterial toxins and drugs all combine to form this new protein molecule and an allergy is the result. Reckeweg points out that during the normal acid phase, which occurs each morning at 3 a.m., these homotoxins become active in the tissues so that a variety of pains occur at this time. Examples are angina, ulcer pains, itching of eczemas and asthma.

The correct resolution of two common diseases may be mentioned as examples of inflammation which retraces in the healthy manner. Reckeweg points out that in asthma, histamine is involved in all phases and initiates the inflammation which deals with the toxins. Dyspnoea (difficult breathing) coincides with the impregnation of toxins and then bronchitic asthma ensues. With correct treatment this retraces back to the sputum excretion phase. In pneumonia, the pneumococcal bacteria release the enzyme hyaluronidase which dissolves the bronchial exudation (excretion). With the help of herbs, homoeopathics and other natural approaches, the toxins and mucus are then able to be eliminated from the congested lungs. Sulphonimides and other antibiotics suppress this resolution. In clinical practice over seventeen years, I have never found that pneumonia develops when bronchial infections are assisted by natural therapies. The excretion phase is thus stimulated so that any dangerous consolidation of the lung does not take place.

The explanation by Reckeweg of autoimmune disease development is very logical. Antibodies are formed in response to the formation of the wild peptides following suppression of inflammation. They attack these similarly structured molecules (wild peptides) which are now deeply embedded in normal tissue in an attempt to remove this foreign material. It appears that the antibodies are attacking the normal tissues. The tissue, however, is not normal as it contains the foreign protein molecules previously described. Thus, we can see that autoimmune disease may result from the suppression of the inflammatory process and perhaps this is why autoimmune diseases involving the kidneys (nephritis), nervous system (multiple sclerosis) and muscles (muscular dystrophy) are on the increase.

Bechamp versus Pasteur

Turning from the observations of Reckeweg, who noted the true role of bacteria in the disease process, we look backwards in time to the discovery of germs or bacteria. This discovery is usually attributed to Louis Pasteur. However, the true discoverer was a medical scientist by the name of Pierre Antoine Bechamp. If the teachings of Bechamp had been followed, medicine would have a different orientation and be more inclined towards a naturopathic framework. It is therefore appropriate to investigate this fraud of historical recording of bacterial discoveries, and the bacterial cause and role in the disease process.

Bechamp was born in Lorraine in France in 1816, six years before the famous Pasteur. Of the two men, Bechamp had a far superior academic training and standing. With a degree in pharmacy, and doctorates in science and medicine, he held positions of significance including professor of medical chemistry and pharmacy at Montpellier, and dean of the faculty of medicine at Lille. Pasteur was trained only in pharmacy and chemistry. By means of one of those fortunate political quirks, Pasteur engaged the favour of Napoleon and his court. This provided him with a good income for life without the need of regular work. Bechamp, on the other hand, undertook his prodigious research in his spare time although this extra work did not prevent him outliving Pasteur by many years.

Before briefly outlining some of the experiments of Bechamp and Pasteur, we need to recall the theory of living matter as it was expounded in the nineteenth century. Huxley saw a primary protoplasmic state similar to the white of an egg. Others described this substance as primordial slime resembling mucus. Later, Vinchow thought he saw the cell in the process of organisation, describing it as the basic building block of living matter.

The other significant issue at this time was the phenomenon of fermentation and putrefaction. Scientists did not know how these processes took place and Pasteur and Bechamp both began working on this process. Pasteur is renowned as the first to reveal the cause of fermentation and to have overthrown the idea of spontaneous generation. Literary research indicates that Bechamp was the first both to research the cause of fermentation as being airborne organisms and to publish the material.[3]

In 1854, Bechamp undertook his Beacon experiment in which the presence of bacteria was noted. Cane-sugar was placed in distilled water in a stoppered flask containing a little air. Over some months moulds formed in the flask. No moulds developed in the control flask, containing sugared water without air. It had previously been believed that fermentation could only take place in the presence of albuminoid matter. The moulds when heated with caustic potash gave off ammonia, demonstrating their nitrogenous and organic basis. Results of this experiment were sent to the French academy of science in 1857. Bechamp commented on his experiment to the effect that the transformation undergone by cane-sugar in the presence of moulds may be compared with changes brought about by the enzyme diastase when acting on starch. This implied that the mould acted as a ferment.

Pasteur only commenced experiments of fermentation in 1857. At this time he experimented with a ferment obtained from a medium of sugar, chalk, casien and gluten all mixed in a yeast broth giving a complex solution of albuminoid and a mineral substance. He concluded that a lactic ferment takes birth spontaneously in the liquid, and as he used yeast broth his experiments did not reveal the role of airborne organisms in a completely chemical medium. Later, he undertook experiments omitting the protein matter and concluded well after the publication of Bechamp's experiment that the origin of lactic yeast in these experiments was due to atmospheric air.

The later work by Bechamp deserves mention as it is this work which reveals the gross mistake which modern medicine has perpetuated in the realm of bacteria. He found that heat destroys the activity of the ferment secreted by yeast and moulds of all sorts. In a paper read to the French Academy of Science in 1864, Bechamp coined the term zymase to cover soluble ferments. He was thus probably the first medical scientist to work with enzymes, which are now recognised as an intrinsic part of modern biochemistry.

He was on the way to developing his crowning thesis on microzymas. To explain this thesis adequately, one must remember that the cell at this time was regarded as the smallest anatomical unit. The important discovery had just been made that airborne organisms were responsible for fermentation and putrefaction. Bechamp now went one step further. He discovered that some of the molecular granulations present in cells of all animal tissue are minute living bodies, capable not only of acting as ferments under normal conditions, but also of evolving into bacteria under adverse conditions! In a number of experiments Bechamp and his colleagues observed the transformation of the tiny entities he named microzymas into various types of bacteria. Using polarised light, they observed microzymas evolving through different stages of bacterial growth including rod and spherical shapes. Having isolated dead tissue from airborne organisms, the microzymas were observed to gradually become mobile, gather together in groups and then develop into bacteria. These were then seen to act as fermenting agents until the dead tissue was reduced to its chemical constituents. Further observations revealed that the bacteria reverted back to microzymas, although sometimes in a modified form.

This is a direct parallel to the model presented by Reckeweg. He had drawn attention to the role of bacteria as they released enzymes which in turn released toxins from diseased tissue. Bechamp appears to have observed a similar phenomenon in addition to the observation that the bacteria actually develop from within the tissue under certain conditions. It is often asked why modern medical scientists would not have observed similar phenomena. For many decades it has been the practice to work with dead and stained tissue using particular techniques where enzyme activity would not take place due to the process of electronic microscopy. How many medical scientists have the attitude of watching and waiting with an open mind to see what will happen to live tissue?

The concepts we have about immunity and preventive medicine take on a new colouring when viewed in the light of these observations by Reckeweg and Bechamp. If bacteria can develop from the minute bodies within the cell under certain conditions, what are the conditions which give rise to their morbid evolution? We have already discussed the role of toxins in relation to the role of bacteria. The fact that we label a particular set of symptoms in relation to a fever does not mean that the main cause comes from outside the system.

Bechamp further developed his theory to suggest that the germs of the air were, in fact, evolved from microzymas of dead animals and human remains. He maintained that the earth and environment are laden with microzymas in various stages of development. He used his theory to explain why everyone in an epidemic does not catch the disease, pointing out that if the outside factor was the main criterion everyone would succumb. Here are Bechamp's own words from his book *The Blood and Its Third Anatomical Element*:

> I return to the microzymas. I had described them from the commencement as being chemically and physiologically figured ferments, producers of zymases, which are called soluble ferments and placed in the same category as the figured ferments which are insoluble. Biologically, I distinguished them as being such as by evolution could become vibrionien, (bacterial) a fact which we have seen to be verified in every sense. But in the experiments on spontaneous alterations, or fermentations, wherein microzymas become bacteria, we have seen that these were destroyed and that vibrioniens more and more minute appeared in their place, so that at last there remained only of these bacteria the forms nearest to the microzymas; . . .

and further:

> These researches led to a result of very great importance; it was the demonstration that what was and is still called germs of the air are essentially nothing other than the microzymas of beings which have lived, but have disappeared or are being destroyed before our eyes. In fact, by precise experiments, I have proved that the microzymas of the air are ferments of the same order as those of the chalk, of the rocks, and of those of artificial chalk; only, varying with the places.[4]

In summary, Bechamp was perhaps the first to notice the true role of bacteria in relation to health and disease. He saw the bacteria as intimately related to the biochemistry of living entities and as having a role in reducing dead tissue to simpler chemical consituents. We now look briefly at the work of another extraordinary pioneer who also made observations which relate to the changing role of bacteria in relation to toxaemia, health and disease.

Reich, Energy Vesicles and 'T Bacilli'

Reich was a medical scientist from Germany who specialised first in psychiatry before working in the field of microbiology. In the late 1930s while working in Norway, Reich discovered the existence of an energy which he named Orgone. He devised the following protocol for releasing this energy. Earth or sand particles were heated to a white incandescence and then plunged into a sterile solution of potassium chloride and broth. On examination under a magnification of 2–3000x, blue shimmering vesicles were seen to develop almost immediately in the solution. These vesicles were found to measure one micron across and stained gram positive. Reich was careful to distinguish the movement of these particles from the random type which is known as Brownian movement and which results from outside influences on particles. Named by Reich as 'blue bions', the energy vesicles were found to have a particular rhythm to the stopping and starting of their pulsation.

The cultures of blue bions were kept in the laboratory for some time and it was noticed that they gave off a type of radiation which appeared like a blue fog in the laboratory. This same type of energy was seen as being emitted from anyone working in the laboratory for some time. The eyes of people in the laboratory became irritated as if exposed to intense sunlight and skin was tanned as from sunlight. An attempt to measure the radiation by the usual means with an electroscope was unsuccessful. Strange to relate, the radiation could be measured indirectly by first exposing rubber gloves to the cultures. The reader will be reminded of the effect of rubber and polymers in relation to the etheric force of Reid. Reich appears to have found a way of releasing the etheric force from matter and of concentrating this force.

After further experiments Reich found that this type of energy was present everywhere throughout space, and he concluded, as have philosophers from the East for many centuries, that it originally emanates from the sun. Reich built simple instruments for accumulating the energy for use in therapy. These orgone accumulators consisted of layers of metal and organic substance like wood. The inside layer was always metal and the outside organic. Numerous trials with cancer patients indicated that when placed for a period in the accumulator each day the haemoglobin content of the blood in anaemic patients improved dramatically without iron therapy over a few weeks.

Reich investigated the blood microscopically to assess what was taking place in the orgone accumulator. Healthy blood was broken down by autoclaving and then cultured. On observing the blood under high magnification, the blood was now found to have given way to blue bions. The bions appeared to be a materialised form of the ether energy. When the same process was undertaken with blood from diseased persons it was found to reveal a mass of bacteria which Reich called 'T bacilli'. In later experiments Reich showed how the blue bions and 'T bacilli' had a type of polarity, each being inimical to the other. 'Blue bions' had the capacity to draw energy away from the 'T bacilli'. The diseased patients in the orgone accumulators had their blood recharged with energy or ether, and this manifested at blood level as the increasing presence of blue bions instead of 'T bacilli'.

'T bacilli' were found in small numbers in the blood and tissues of most persons but as pathology increased large numbers developed. The bacteria are only 0·2 microns in length and therefore can only be observed under a magnification of over 2000X. In keeping with the basic principles of natural healing, Reich understood chronic disease as a gradual degenerative and putrefactive process of body tissues, following a contraction of the autonomic nervous system (ANS). His chain of disease involved emotional repression, then a shrinking of the ANS, diminishing of vital energy, concluding in breakdown of body protein which resulted in putrefaction with development of large quantities of 'T bacilli'. The blue bions were observed to have a paralysing effect on the 'T bacilli' but as disease progressed the 'T bacilli' gradually predominated.

In his book *The Cancer Biopathy*, further observations and

experiments are described in which Reich observed that following the disappearance of blue bions in degenerating tissues, club-like and caudate-form cells with motility develop. These were seen as the forerunner of cancer cells. Slow jerky movement with rhythmic contraction of these cells was observed with a magnification of over 3000X. These cells were noted to infiltrate and cause disintegration of surrounding tissue which later develops into cancer tissue. The final stage was seen to be liquefaction of plasma and development of flowing ameboid protozoa, and at this stage life usually terminates.[5]

The observations of Reckeweg as he described the inflammation and disease process finds an echo in the work of Reich. Reckeweg was describing the role of a different class of bacteria in his description of the inflammatory process from those observed by Reich. As a medical scientist and naturopath he was more concerned with the move towards health of the organism and the process as it takes place in fever and inflammation. It is notable that both Bechamp and Reich observed the evolution of bacteria from one form to another according to the health of the host. Once again, modern science tends to ignore the flow of events and observes bacteria in isolation from their previous or future state. There is no general recognition of disease as a process which develops from within the person. Reich and Bechamp were both interested in the putrefactive processes in nature and how this manifested in human disease as a gradual dissolution involving changing bacterial status from within the body.

In the work of Reich, we have an extraordinary parallel to the work of Bechamp. Both scientists observed bacteria as existing and developing from within the cells rather than as an infection from outside. In terms of basic naturopathic philosophy there is also the finding by Reich that diminishing energy or vitality (orgone) within a living organism is in direct proportion to the increase of bacteria. We also note the relation between orgone and the work of Reid, who examined the force called ether as possibly influencing all living organisms. Both scientists saw 'ether'/'orgone' as permeating all space and as having a direct influence on happenings at the cellular level.

As with the work of Bechamp, people ask why have not other medical scientists noticed 'blue bions' and 'T bacilli' and the development of the bacterial and protozoal forms noted by Reich in the pathological process. As long as medical scientists continue to see diseases as isolated entities which are believed to come from without the organism, they will continue to make observations in isolation to the flow of health and disease. Other medical scientists with a broad frame of reference have duplicated the work of Reich. I have observed the fairly simple procedure of cultivating 'blue bions' from healthy blood. Laboratory work in relation to disease and health tends to take place according to our frame of reference.

As a psychiatrist, Reich was particularly interested in the emotional state of his cancer patients and how this related to degenerative disease processes. He saw biological pulsation as the fundamental healthy quality of living organisms. He saw emotional repression, particularly in the sexual sphere, as causing a gradual contraction of the ANS with coincident lack of normal energy flow to all tissues. Perhaps in his emphasis on the orgasmic reflex, Reich overstated the sexual aspect of health, and ignored the broader relation of energy flow and health which has been explored in Eastern philosophy for thousands of years. It is interesting how pioneers, in spite of their breadth of vision and mental illumination, tend to have 'blinkers' in one particular area. The relation between psychic health and energy flow, whether we call it by the Sanskrit term of 'prana', or whether we use the terms 'orgone', 'ether' or just plain vitality, is all-important. In the work of Rudolf Steiner we find perhaps the only model which has systematically blended the inner psychic constitution with the two poles of acute and chronic disease.

Anthroposophical Medical Approach to Inflammation and Toxins

Rudolf Steiner, a mystic and philosopher, developed a unique system called anthroposophical medicine which is flourishing, particularly in Europe today. Unusual as the following model may seem in some respects, it is of note that a number of orthodox physicians have trained in this school and obtain excellent results using herbs, homoeopathics and other drugless approaches to inflammation and toxaemia. In anthroposophical medicine the two physiological poles are called the nerve sense pole and the metabolic pole. In disease, these two processes become respectively the sclerosing and inflammation principles. In health, the upper pole (sensory) and lower or metabolic activities are in balance and augment each other. These activities include the psychic dimensions of the individual and therefore the whole person is involved. The sensory pole is the vehicle for the feeling and thinking nature of the person, and for healthy metabolism and digestion this needs to be integrated with the physical body in an harmonious way.

According to doctors of anthroposophical medicine, allergies arise from inadequate digestion of food and chemicals taken into the body when the metabolic pole is not directed adequately by the nerve sensory system. The inflammation process takes place as the result of re-entry by the astral or feeling nature so as to penetrate the physical body more fully, stimulating digestion of toxins more adeqately, thus restoring balance. The sclerosing principle has the opposite effect from inflammation when it influences the body too strongly in the absence of sufficient activity from the metabolic pole. The catabolic effect which is necessary in a moderate degree to break down a substance taken into the body then assumes degenerative proportions and manifests through deposition of crystals and hardening of body structures—sclerosis. In the final absence of any inflammatory influence and an excess of the sclerosing principle, cancer takes place.[6]

This particular model varies from the previous one because the psychic processes of the individual are understood to have a direct bearing on both inflammatory and degenerative processes. The metabolic and digestive processes of the body which correctly break down and assimilate the food result from correct balance of thoughts, emotions and feelings as they substand or automatically direct the physical metabolism of the body. A lack of integration between the feeling nature and the body—in other words, disowned feelings—is understood to cause a move towards the degenerative pole of existence with cancer as the final outcome.

Once again, the inflammatory process is seen to reverse the degenerative sclerotic diseases and anthroposophical medicine is directed in cases of malignant disease to awakening the inflammatory process. To this end, not only are the physical herbs and homoeopathic medicines administered but the patient is engaged in painting, music and movements to music (eurhythmy) to engage the feeling nature in bodily processes. Allergies are seen as resulting from a weakness in the digestive and metabolic processes, whereby food or environmental toxins remain 'undigested', thus giving rise to foreign proteins which then act as allergens. Like the previous model, allergies are not seen as something which affects the person from outside by chance or from genetic factors alone.

We can also refer to the model of Bevan Reid in Chapter 4. His two poles of coherence and differentiation may coincide with the sclerosis and inflammation of the anthroposophical school of thought. When molecules become too tightly stacked or coherent in tissues, Reid sees the possibility of cancer. He sees inflammation as a very good example of turbulence which can break down the coherence and restore the balance or flow of energies through the organism.

The work of the scientists described in this chapter is controversial within the scientific community, but this has always been the case always for the leading edge of science. All these scientists, apart from Rudolf Steiner, have been trained within the orthodox framework of medical science existing at their time of life. Each has been involved at the practical level of health and disease, and each has provided a challenge for us to see the synthesis which is apparent from their various contributions.

CHAPTER 10

Subjective Factors in Toxaemia and Devitalisation

Why are many natural therapists interested in Eastern philosophy, meditation and related topics? How can we influence our health from psychic levels of being? What relationship does the etheric body have to our psyche and how do the etheric body and its energy centres, called chakras, influence health?

The Etheric Realm — Focus of Natural Therapies

We have explored the meaning of energy and vitality in Chapters 2 and 3. It is appropriate now to describe the possible mechanism for reception and transmission of subtle energies throughout the physical body. These concepts have originally come from the East but are now widely accepted by an increasing number of Western people. In particular, natural therapists tend to study this topic because the focus of therapies like herbs, vitamins, homoeopathy, and acupuncture appears to be beyond the physical body and in the etheric realm.

From this template or etheric body which is found to mediate between the more subjective parts of our psyche and the physical body, the pattern for growth and regrowth or regeneration appears to develop. The word regeneration here is used in its broadest sense to mean the healing process. Having observed how our clientele first responds in the healing process with an experience of increased vitality and energy, the therapist is naturally curious to explore those medical philosophies which emphasise this aspect. Enough medical evidence has been described in Chapters 2 and 3 to provide for the possible validity of viewing the human body as basically influenced in health and disease by energy fields. At this point, these fields can be expressed only in electrical terms.

The most lucid and informative teaching about the structure of the subtle body or constitution comes from the Trans-Himalayan teaching which was first brought to the West around the turn of the century with the writings of H. P. Blavatsky.[1] This same teaching was carried on by A. A. Bailey for thirty years between 1920 and 1950.[2] During and since that time, many writers, teachers and students have created their own versions and compilations which, with a few exceptions, add nothing to the significance of the original versions. A quick scan through lists of leading publishing houses will reveal the great popularity of these esoteric subjects today. No treatise on holistic healing should avoid some inclusion of this teaching on the etheric body.

Functions of the Etheric Body

The etheric body has three main functions. First, it is the mediator between the subjective nature of emotions, feelings, thoughts, spiritual essence and our physical brain. Secondly, it receives, assimilates and distributes energy or prana from the sun to all parts of the physical body. Thirdly, it provides the pattern for growth and regrowth or healing for all the physical cells and tissues of the body.

During the last few decades of materialistic attitudes, it has generally been accepted that the mind is a product of the brain. Only recently, with the gathering of information from out-of-the-body experiences including those of near death, and with recent research and speculation on brain function, more thought has been given to other models for mind/body interaction.[3] The etheric body is that subtle part of the physical anatomy and physiology which receives and transmits thoughts, feelings and spiritual impulses to the physical brain consciousness.

What happens if this important connecting link becomes hardened, thickened or dissipated? It is here that life-style and natural therapies become very relevant. Factors which have a direct influence on the etheric body are fresh air, sunlight, nutrition, walking, relaxation and meditation. The etheric level of our being can be considerably modified over a lifetime either in a positive or negative sense. A person born with poor health heredity and with inadequate care as a child will tend to grow up with various miasms (see next chapter) grafted onto their etheric vehicle. As a young adult, they may start to take responsibility for their own health. Gradually their etheric nature will become refined, strong and tensile as they improve nutrition, work on their psychological stresses and develop a healthy life-style. This includes relaxation, moderate sunbathing and exercise plus a meditative or reflective approach to life. The immune system will become much stronger and tendency to infections will disappear. Greater stamina for work, both physical and mental, will take place.

We can also visualise the reverse situation. A person born with a good inherited constitution and given reasonable care in childhood may develop habits for junk food and smoking in late teens. They tend to keep late hours and dissipate themselves through regular parties where liberal amounts of alcohol are consumed. Their erratic life-style places psychological stress on the working life and various emotional strains develop. The etheric web is gradually thickened and coarsened and energy which normally flows through to the nerves and brain is diminished. A train of depression is engendered and the higher impulses which would tend to encourage the person to become integrated are unable to penetrate through to the brain consciousness.

A vicious circle is established whereby the worse the life-style becomes, the more difficult it is for the person to break the destructive cycle. Natural therapies can be of great assist-ance in breaking this cycle and giving the person a fresh start to etheric health while they are working on their life-style. Vitamin B-complex is used for general nerve tone; vitamin C for detoxification from chemicals, tobacco and alcohol; herbs for cleansing of the lymphatic system, and Bach flower remedies and other flower essences for emotional imbalance. Both homoeopathic remedies and flower essences have a direct effect on the etheric body, while vitamins and herbs have a reflex or indirect action.

Individuals tend to move either towards a thickening of the etheric web or towards dissipation. In the latter case, the problem can manifest as a nervous breakdown or extreme exhaustion with nervous stress. Alternatively, there may be a thickening in an area corresponding to particular physical organs such as the brain or liver, and a thinning in another area. If the etheric is locked too closely to the physical, an over-stimulation of the nervous system will take place with nervous stress and tension, and insomnia. This is more likely to occur in those people with a dissipation of the etheric energies and structure.

In observing the second function of energy reception and distribution, this ability will depend on the health and type of the etheric vehicle. Some people absorb and distribute energy much more effectively than others and this in turn conditions the nervous system and all bodily functions. The energy is received through three distributing centres in the etheric body called the pranic triangle. These centres consist of the spleen centre, a centre near the diaphragm and one between the shoulder blades. Due to the life-style and clothes of Westerners during the last few centuries, these centres have often become shrunken and misplaced. The apprehension of energy is not always adequate. Moderate sunbathing and emphasis on out-door activities is improving the etheric health of many people.

The actual density of the etheric vehicle, apart from the pranic triangle, varies considerably from person to person. A loose structure will cause energy to be rapidly absorbed and as easily lost, causing the individual to feel depleted. This situation tends to develop in some Westerners who live in tropical zones. People born in these areas are inclined to be more adapted to the situation. General life-style habits such as nutrition, pollution, taking of addictive substances, and psychological state will condition the etheric and its capacity for energy reception.

If the etheric is too loosely connected with the physical body, there will be a lack of energy flowing through the physical nervous system with exhaustion, and weakness in particular organs. A temporary manifestation, with withdrawal of the etheric from the physical, occurs partially in laryngitis and more systemically with a general anaesthetic. In the loss of consciousness during fainting, epilepsy or general anaesthesia, the body is temporarily 'senseless'. This is a colloquial but expressive phrase for an impotent state of the central nervous system. The autonomic or more automatic part of the nervous system continues with those activities which are not normally under the control of the will, such as heartbeat, breathing, and hormonal secretion.

The third function of the etheric is to provide the pattern or scaffolding around which growth or regrowth takes place. It is this aspect which was discussed earlier in Chapters 2 and 3 in terms of the observations made by the medical scientists Burr, Reich, Becker, Sheldrake and Reid. This particular role of the etheric vehicle is intimately associated with the effect of natural medicine. Natural therapies strengthen, refine and balance the etheric pattern and energies plus enhancing the relation between the etheric and physical bodies. This results in the experience of greater vitality, immunity, relaxation and a general sense of well-being.

Structure of the Etheric Body

The etheric body is sometimes defined as consisting of one long filament of light/energy which takes the form of a web of light underlying the physical structure. The conditioning factor derived from life-style has been mentioned. Behind this factor is a more significant one. Our etheric substance is conditioned from the level of being on which our consciousness is focused. It is therefore necessary to include here a brief description of the seven levels of consciousness which form the field for human living and adventures.

It is accepted by most students of Eastern philosophy that there are seven planes in the universe. Starting at the bottom (which is closest to our brain consciousness), we have the three planes which concern our personality life: the physical, astral and mental planes. These involve our bodily sensations, feelings/emotions, and thoughts. The main difference between Eastern and Western psychology is that in the East a definite mechanism for thoughts and feelings is described. There is not the problem, therefore, as to what part of the brain thoughts and feelings are attached. A person is understood to have a vehicle for feelings and another for thoughts, which interpenetrate the etheric/physical body. The brain is seen more as a transmitter or computer terminal rather than as a thinking, reasoning and memorising organ in itself.

Transpersonal, out-of-the-body, near-death and after-death experiences are able to be seen in a different perspective by those indiviuals who have studied and accepted Eastern teachings. The feeling and thinking entity we understand as a human being is understood to cycle repeatedly around these three lower planes through the process called reincarnation. The qualities from each incarnation are stored within the permanent spiritual body which is called the soul body. The soul resides on the higher levels of the mental plane and increasingly conditions the etheric/physical consciousness once an individual begins to take responsibility for their personality in all its facets. Meditation and other spiritual practices are aids to gaining soul consciousness which eventually brings perfect health as the soul becomes fused with the personality life.

The four higher planes of the universe moving upwards are the Buddhic, Atmic, Monadic, and Anupadaka or plane of the Divine. The Buddhic plane is the focus of love/wisdom and of all spiritually enlightened beings. The Atmic plane is the plane of spiritual will, and the Monadic plane is that on which our highest spiritual essence resides. These four highest planes are called the cosmic ethers and as individuals open themselves through meditation and service to these levels, they gradually condition the individual etheric body until it is able to transmit these spiritual energies into the environment. All great teachers, like Buddha and Christ, are transmitters of spiritual energies into the environment through their perfected physical, astral and mental forms.

Our model encompasses, therefore, the concept that our physical health is conditioned by the etheric body which in turn is conditioned by whatever level or levels our consciousness is focused on. We can envisage a continual transmission of energies from one level to another, with the physical body as the final receiving station.

The means of transmitting energies through the etheric body occurs through centres called chakras, which is a Sanskrit word meaning wheel. These centres are found within the etheric substance and are formed from the strands of energy crossing many times. Where the energy crosses twenty-one times, the seven major centres are formed. There are also a number of secondary centres such as those described involving the pranic triangle. Other secondary centres include those associated with the eyes, ears, digestive organs, and kidneys. Hundreds of tiny centres are represented by the traditional acupuncture points. Each of the main seven centres is associated with one of the seven planes of consciousness and each on the physical end, externalises itself through an endocrine gland. Our physical health is intimately related to the function and balance of the energy centres.

Problems with the energy centres can take place in several ways. There can be a problem in the psyche involving thoughts and feelings and this will distort the centre from the inner side. There can be a problem at the outlet into the physical body and this may be a reflex action back from an inherited problem with the endocrine gland involved with a particular centre. An over- or under-activity in one centre will affect all the other centres to some extent. The centres with their respective glands and associated anatomical structures are in the diagram 'The Energy Centres in Man'. In the average person, the centres below the diaphragm are the most active and these correspond to the personality life and to sensations, feelings and concrete thoughts. The centres above the diaphragm gradually become active as we resolve our personality problems and invoke inclusive love, intelligent discriminatory activity and spiritual will into our lives.

All health problems involve the centres to some extent and are a major conditioning factor within the etheric body for physical conditions. They are responsible for the channelling of energy into the associated gland, organ and tissues and therefore too much or too little energy will affect the physiology, anatomy and biochemistry. The importance of balancing the centres through a rhythmic life-style, healthy psyche and right attitude towards life cannot be overestimated.

The Centres and Their Function in Health and Disease

We will examine the chakras in terms firstly of human development and unfoldment, and secondly in terms of health problems which can arise when unfoldment is blocked, jerky or premature. This model will enable the reader to see the relationship between the chakras, planes, glands, organs and disease states. We need to remember a chain when thinking of the effect of the chakras on health and disease and this chain flows as follows: thoughts − feelings − chakra − nervous system − endocrine gland − blood − tissues. There can be a problem at any point in the chain with reflex action occurring in other parts of the flow. We will trace the seven main chakras from below upwards and present a general overview. Books by Karagulla, Tansley and Lansdowne will provide the reader with further information in this area.[4]

The Energy Centres

ASSOCIATED GLAND ORGAN AND BODY SYSTEM

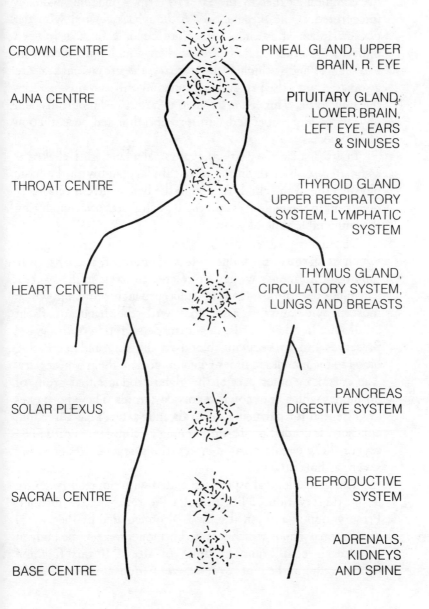

CROWN CENTRE — PINEAL GLAND, UPPER BRAIN, R. EYE

AJNA CENTRE — PITUITARY GLAND, LOWER BRAIN, LEFT EYE, EARS & SINUSES

THROAT CENTRE — THYROID GLAND UPPER RESPIRATORY SYSTEM, LYMPHATIC SYSTEM

HEART CENTRE — THYMUS GLAND, CIRCULATORY SYSTEM, LUNGS AND BREASTS

SOLAR PLEXUS — PANCREAS DIGESTIVE SYSTEM

SACRAL CENTRE — REPRODUCTIVE SYSTEM

BASE CENTRE — ADRENALS, KIDNEYS AND SPINE

The Base Chakra. The base chakra is associated with the physical plane and is situated posterior to the spine in the area of coccyx (tail-bone). This chakra houses the fire commonly called by the Sanskrit term 'Kundalini', which is interpreted as the serpent fire. Although associated with the physical plane, this chakra does not become fully developed until all the other chakras are awakened and controlled. The base centre and its higher counterpart, the crown chakra, are associated with the principle of spiritual will and this includes the will to be. This lowest centre is both psychologically and physiologically associated with preservation and perpetuation of the species.

In its association with the physical plane, this chakra is associated with birth on the physical plane and with the basic physical life of the child. Although the base centre is relatively quiescent in the child it is still the basis for preservation during this vulnerable time of growth.

The associated endocrine glands are the adrenal glands which sit on top of the kidneys. It is of interest that they secrete important hormones which are related to stress in the system. The inner part of the gland (medulla) produces adrenalin which most people know is associated with the fright or flight syndrome. In other words, the hormone secretion of this gland preserves life by reducing blood to the skin and increasing blood to the muscles in times when immediate flight is necessary. The cortex or outer part of the gland produces that group of hormones which are known as corticosteroids. These hormones are essential for balancing minerals and water. Like adrenalin, cortisone is needed in life-threatening circumstances caused by severe allergic reaction as in insect stings, severe infection, and severe asthma attacks.

The psychological aspect associated with this energy centre is the preservation of life through the reproductive instinct. Preservation in a physical sense is also mediated by the associated adrenal glands which secrete hormones to keep the body in balance or equilibrium in times of stress. If this function becomes diminished or over-active various problems arise.

Unused adrenalin from modern stress often no longer allows for any physical outlet and is now suspected as a contributing factor to cancer. More commonly, this type of stress may manifest as high blood pressure and this essential form of hypertension may be quite unrelated to hardening of the arteries. It often appears in people in their twenties. In these cases we could say that the base chakra is over-active.

Related physical organs and tissues for this centre are the kidneys, adrenal glands, ureters, bladder, spine, and genital organs. Certain types of high blood pressure connected with kidney problems result from imbalance in this centre. Likewise, very low blood pressure may be caused by under-activity of the centre. Addison's disease is an extreme example whereby the blood pressure is low enough to be life-threatening and it is now thought that this disease may be an autoimmune disorder where destructive antibodies cause structural changes in the kidney substance. Physical problems with the genital organs, kidneys and spine belong to this centre but sexual problems which are usually psychological relate more properly to the next chakra upwards—the sacral centre.

The Sacral Centre. This centre is situated at the base of the lumbar spine and is associated with the subtle part of the physical called the etheric level. It is associated therefore with the life force or vital energy which substands the physical body. In the growing child this chakra is developed from birth to the age of seven years. During this stage, preservation of life is the main emphasis and the child is mainly concerned with food and comfort. It is a time of life when the etheric vehicle or subtle part of the physical body becomes organised and there is a big emphasis on physical growth and development. The developing of healthy immunity is intimately related to the health of the etheric during these years. For this reason natural therapists place great stress on the use of appropriate herbs, vitamins and homoeopathic remedies throughout these years to regulate, strengthen and purify the etheric against any inherited problems. This does not mean that the etheric cannot be helped at a later stage but it is much easier during the first seven years of life.

The psychological aspects of this energy centre relate to our appetites for food, comfort and sex. The endocrine glands related to the sacral centre are the gonads—testes in the male and ovaries in the female. Associated physical organs and tissues are the reproductive organs in both sexes, and the legs. There are related minor centres in the area of hips, knees and feet. Under- or over-activity of the sacral centre can result in problems with any of these organs. Examples of diseases include ovarian and testicular cysts and tumours, blocked fallopian tubes, enlarged prostate gland, uterine fibroids, and cancer of these organs.

In terms of our psychological and spiritual growth, we gradually learn to control and direct creatively the etheric/physical energies within both ourselves and the environment. A good clue to the activity of this centre is indicated by our ability to attract and handle money. Under-activity of the sacral chakra results not only in types of sexual impotence but produces an inability to earn money and to use it for either selfish or unselfish purposes. Appropriately the metal gold is a symbol for the sacral centre. Over-activity may give excessive sexual activity, and an over-emphasis on material values generally. All sexual problems are related to imbalance in this centre.

It is interesting to observe how the emphasis on the centres change in humanity as a whole and how this affects our health. Over the last few decades since the Victorian era, humanity has been released from many sexual taboos and much psychological ill health from sexual repression and suppression has been resolved. A section of humanity has now allowed the pendulum to swing in the opposite direction and is devoted to sexual gratification divorced from considerations of any deeper aspects of relationships. Certain practices to enhance sexual stimulus to extraordinary degrees are used. These practices have been demonstrated to diminish the health of the immune system. There is speculation that the increasing epidemic of AIDS

(Acquired Immune Deficiency Syndrome), while not now restricted to persons indulging in promiscuous behaviour, may certainly have been given a good initial boost by such activity. AIDS is related to the sacral centre, as are all infectious venereal diseases. Other infectious problems related to this centre involve genital warts and herpes.

On a global scale this centre involves pockets of wealth which indicate a lack of sharing of planetary resources. The imbalance of the sacral centre within humanity is expressed in the millions of starving persons who, in most cases, are also without shelter and comforts. This imbalance in the planetary life energy is connected with infectious epidemics on a broad scale and also with weather eccentricities such as tornadoes and hurricanes. When the majority within humanity have controlled the sacral centre there will be universal health, sharing and prosperity. In other words, an even flow of vitality and life-force (as symbolised by money) throughout the planet will eventuate.

The higher counterpart of the sacral chakra is the throat centre and when this becomes active, the energies of the sacral centre are drawn upwards and regulated by the throat chakra. The energies in the sacral chakra are then used to provide the physical means of expressing mental creativity and for grounding our schemes. It is important therefore that the sacral energies are not suppressed but wisely used in service to the whole.

The Solar Plexus. The average person is focused through this centre and it is therefore a major conditioning factor for disease in modern man. The solar plexus is situated at the level of the twelfth thoracic and first lumbar vertabrae and relates to the astral plane, providing the door to this level of feelings/emotions. In the growing child, an awareness of this level of consciousness peaks between the ages of seven and fourteen years. For this reason, some educators have emphasised the need for children in this age group to develop fully all those artistic activities which can impose a healthy rhythm in the feeling nature. In Rudolf Steiner schools for instance, music, painting and other artistic activities are emphasised and strictly mental pursuits are not stressed until secondary school. This is to prevent a blockage in the normal astral rhythms of the child which in later life could seriously affect the flow of energies resulting in disease.

It is obvious that many persons become stuck in this stage of emotional development. Over the last twenty years a growing awareness has taken place within humanity for the need to unblock emotions and allow feelings to be expressed freely. We have witnessed the explosion of therapy groups conducted by both trained and untrained persons. As with the greater awareness of the sacral centre and its sexual expression, humanity has in some instances gone overboard in expressing freedom through the solar plexus. The great emphasis on sensationalism in art, theatre, film and television programmes, plus the violence of contemporary life generally, indicates an unbridled solar plexus activity.

As with the sacral centre, it is in the consideration of the higher counterpart to the solar plexus that we can see wise control without suppression of this centre. This will be discussed under the heart centre. The solar plexus responds to every feeling and desire no matter how subtle. It often works in close marriage with the sacral centre so that the average person is ruled by desires related to material possessions and to those appetites discussed in terms of the sacral chakra. More subtle desires involve prestige, ambitions, recognition, and we can even include here desire for a spiritual experience and teacher. No wonder, with the modern emphasis on material assets and values, that the average person is classed as a solar/sacral individual.

The solar plexus acts as a clearing house for all the minor chakras and for the major chakras below the diaphragm. As the energies are raised up past the diaphragm there is a temporary period of great disturbance often involving problems with the associated organs of the digestion. Once the personality becomes integrated, the solar plexus gathers up the energies and they are passed on to the centres above the diaphragm.

The endocrine gland associated with this centre is the pancreas, a major digestive organ which has both an exocrine (outer) and endocrine or hormonal secretion. The pancreatic juice is a digestive secretion which deals with fats, carbohydrates and proteins. The hormone insulin is responsible for balancing blood-sugar levels, and if insufficient, the condition known as diabetes results. In general we could say that if the energy flowing through the solar plexus is insufficient, the digestive organs will be underactive and the food will not be digested or assimilated correctly. This can lead to all kinds of allergies and problems from the undigested food acting as an irritant in the body. Apart from the pancreas, the liver, gall-bladder, stomach, small intestine, and autonomic nervous system are all closely related to the solar plexus.

In terms of health problems, rather than the centre being completely over- or under-active, the action of the centre is often jerky. This gives an imbalance to all the digestive activities and, as a typical example, explains why it is so hard to stabilise some diabetics. Another classical example would be diarrhoea alternating with constipation and the modern medical catch-phrases of spastic colon and irritable bowel syndrome are in keeping with solar plexus irregularities. Other common problems stemming from the solar plexus include gall-stones, stomach ulcers, ulcerative colitis, dyspepsia, flatulence, colic, and various problems associated with assimilation and absorption. Many people also have pain in the area of the solar plexus although no organic cause can be found. This is usually a cramp in the centre itself and is common in children between the ages of five and nine years. Bach flower remedies are excellent for this problem.

_____ CASE HISTORY _____

The following case history is a good example to illustrate the relationship between the solar plexus chakra and digestion. Melinda, aged twenty-three, visited our clinic with symptoms of intermittent abdominal pain around the navel and headache. Two months prior to this visit she had suffered food poisoning and we often find that traces of toxins remain in the system even for years afterwards. This can be established by Vega analysis. Melinda's iris had a type of fibre which is classed as neurogenic by the German school and this often indicates psychosomatic factors. The descending colon was distended and darkened according to iris analysis. The Vega analysis showed stress first in the liver, then in the small and large bowel, but the 'biological age' was not sufficiently high to indicate any severity of residual toxins in the system. The case history, observations, Vega analysis and my own perception all indicated the basic cause to be in the solar plexus chakra rather than in the physical digestive processes.

The first month of remedies was weighted towards balancing the nervous system and toning the digestive organs with magnesium phosphate, vitamin B-complex, and homoeopathic remedies for toning liver and bowel and for removing toxins from liver and lymphatic glands. On her return visit after two weeks Melinda reported no improvement. The remedies were changed to give much more emphasis to the nervous aspect and to balancing solar plexus chakra. To this end, Bach flowers and specific homoeopathic remedies were included and the magnesium phosphate, B-complex and digestive tonic repeated. On her third visit, Melinda reported much improvement and only had one solar plexus cramp after an emotional disturbance. The remedies were continued with minor changes.

At the fourth visit, Melinda had not relapsed to her original state but was concerned that she still had some bouts of pain. I was more convinced that the pain was caused by the solar plexus cramping as a result of emotional problems. I started to explain the possible relationship between anxiety, fears, the solar plexus and the pain. Any suggestion that there could be an emotional factor was strongly resisted at first, almost with a degree of belligerence. Just as I felt I was getting nowhere and would have to take a completely new tack, Melinda burst out that it was all her brother's fault. It then transpired that she had a very disturbed brother who was in trouble with the law and quite unmanageable at home. Her privacy and possessions were periodically at risk and this had severely disturbed her.

Discussion between Melinda and her mother about the problem was side-stepped by the mother who took a very philosophical and non-confronting attitude towards her son. Suggestions about regular counselling were made and accepted by both mother and daughter as having possible value. The physical remedies were continued. A few weeks later Melinda rang and said she was quite cured and did not need to come to the clinic again. I asked if she had undergone any counselling and she said it was not necessary as she had decided not to be disturbed by her brother's behaviour.

If the physical aspects of the case had been the only aspects under treatment, even the addition of Bach flower remedies with their direct action on the chakras would have been insufficient in a case like this. There was constant pressure from the subjective aspect of the psyche on the solar plexus and this caused what appeared to be physical pain as it was translated to the nervous system. The food poisoning may have caused some stress on the digestive organs but was used subconsciously by Melinda to avoid confronting the real cause of her discomfort. The last consultation, which focused on the emotional issues, was sufficient to commence a train of psychological insight which resolved the problem.

Aspiration develops gradually from the desires focused in our solar plexus and eventually our aims, desires, ambitions, and goals are directed to the heart centre which, in the esoteric sense, is called the organ of fusion. The transmutation is understood to take place as a result of our reaction to the pressure of life itself and our creative engagement in this process, rather than primarily as a result of meditation and other practices.

The Heart Centre. We are now looking at the centres above the diaphragm which only become active when we take responsibility for our situation in life. This includes the concurrent development of responsibility towards other lives and forms of life in our environment. Therefore, although a possible age for activation of each of this next group may be given, the majority of people are presently stuck in the personality life which expresses itself through the three lower chakras. Still, more people are developing the higher three centres of head, heart and throat.

The heart centre is situated between the fourth and fifth thoracic vertebrae and should not be confused with the nearby minor centres involved with the pranic triangle and the vagus nerve. The level of consciousness associated with this centre is the Buddhic plane of illumination. The heart centre is correspondingly an organ of healing fusion and wisdom. It bestows an inclusive quality of love for which the word empathy can be used rather than sympathy, which belongs to the solar plexus. In other words, it is an unconditional type of love rather than the self-centred love of the personality which flows so easily through the solar plexus. It is a love which gives perfect understanding of the other so that motives stand unveiled and, in the case of the healer, the cause of disease is truly understood.

The developing heart centre within mankind can be seen in all those individuals and groups who respond to group need within their environment. In secular life an expression of this energy will be found manifesting through that individual or individuals who form the heart centre of an organisation—not necessarily a spiritual organisation in the usual sense of the word. This may encompass work in many spheres of life: including work with plants, trees, sea creatures, pollution issues, and various spheres of healing. The heart centre is therefore intimately related to service, provided that such service results from responsibility or the ability to respond to a sensed need. The wisdom aspect associated with the heart is a marriage of head and heart or of discriminating intelligence and love. From this union comes the term 'ability to think in the heart'.

In an age when many people are depressed about the possible future of the human race, it is worth reminding ourselves that until after the last world war the only obvious well-known philanthropic groups were the Red Cross and the Salvation Army. If we reflect on the enormous number of networks which today are devoted to both humanitarian work and service to the lower kingdoms in nature, we realise the increasing potential for joyful living manifested by an increasing number of individuals.[5]

The endocrine gland related to the heart is the thymus gland, which is situated in the chest just above the heart. Only comparatively recently has the important role of this gland in immunity been perceived. It produces the T–lymphocytes which deal with unwanted viruses and other bodies such as cancer cells. In all immune deficiency disease (of which AIDS is only one) the thymus gland is an important factor. The stimulation of the thymus gland may be an important factor for immunity through correct attitudes to life and through particular forms of meditation.

Allowing energy to flow through the heart chakra also enhances psychic immunity and prevents the common problem of devitalisation through the solar plexus chakra. This is especially important for healers to understand as the inclusive, magnetic and radiatory love characteristic of the heart chakra prevents the common occurrence of 'burn-out'. The latter problem relates to nervous collapse as a result of working too strongly through the solar plexus centre and when we have developed the heart centre, its companion centre—the solar plexus—is brought into harmony and balance.

Heart, blood and circulatory disease is obviously connected with imbalance through the heart chakra and certain forms of lung disease are also included. Other associated tissues are the two breasts. The vagus nerve is also under the control of the heart centre. Examples of diseases are coronary artery disease, valvular problems, aneurisms, varicose veins, palpitations and other arhythmias, and lung disorders including cancer. The energy of the heart centre draws up the energies in the solar plexus and transmutes these energies so that they can be used for the good of the whole. During the interim period, there will be a swing of energies between heart and solar plexus and it is at this time that heart and digestive problems, particularly of a functional nature, can take place.

The Throat Centre. This chakra is situated behind the spine between the seventh cervical and first thoracic vertebrae. It relates to mental creativity in comparison with the sacral centre—the lower counterpart which expresses physical creativity. The corresponding level of consciousness is the lower part of the mental plane which is the home of all our thoughts and physical creativity. The throat centre becomes active as the mind develops. A parallel time of growth is between the ages of fourteen and twenty-one years, a time when the most serious period of study is usually upon us. As the mind gains facility with using thought processes, this centre develops and gives the ability to plan and design. The blueprint is thus provided for perhaps a garden, house, city, musical composition, poem, or piece of literature. The sacral centre provides the etheric energy which includes the finance, and ability to attract the physical means for expression of the plan.

We are all familiar with impractical idealists and these are persons in which there is not the necessary balance between throat and sacral chakra. This can be a stage one goes through when the throat chakra is first stimulated and the sacral centre initially under-active for a period. There can be a coincident fanatical stage which a person can go through in an attempt to discipline the life through controlling the sacral centre. All kinds of strict diets, the practice of celibacy and other physical regimes are practised until it is realised that it is through the control of the astral nature that true freedom comes and not by enforced physical disciplines. A more balanced and rhythmic life-style will then flourish without the rigidity of physical disciplines.

When observing humanity as a whole there is considerable evidence that the throat chakra has awakened on a large scale. This is seen through the emphasis on creativity, adult education programmes and the increasing tendency for everyone to attend workshops, classes and to go on developing creative skills throughout their life. In the third world countries, there has been a preliminary attempt to educate the masses and this is a new event this century.

The gland in front of the throat, called the thyroid, is the endocrine expression of this energy centre. It is responsible for metabolic activities and when energy is slow or suppressed in this area we have an under-active or hypothyroid condition with a slowing down of metabolism, weight gain, slowness of mind and all activities. Alternatively, too much energy flowing through this gland from an over-active mind can cause hyperthyroidism which can raise the blood pressure and cause general nervousness, insomnia, sweating and, in some cases, severe palpitations (tachycardia) which endanger the heart. Associated structures with this energy centre are the vocal chords, pharynx, larynx, bronchial tubes, mouth, tongue, upper lungs, shoulders, arms, hands and the lymphatic system.

Women passing through menopause frequently suffer problems in this centre due to energy shifts from the ovaries upwards. They may become very nervous with hot flushes, palpitations, and weight losses, or they may swing the other way and gain weight while becoming very sluggish mentally and physically. In either case there is a problem with how to use energies creatively in a wise and balanced manner. The first group of women are suddenly imbued with too much energy as the sacral centre changes its role when menstruation ceases. The energy may have no proper creative outlet and may work back onto the system causing over-stimulation. In the second group, there is usually a lack of mental development and the women have not bothered to develop the mind for their own self-expression during their thirties and forties. When the sacral centre changes during menopause there is no input from other levels and both sacral and throat centre become too sluggish.

In the psychological sense this chakra relates to creative thought. Forms of depression in both sexes and lack of creative outlets can be an indication of a sluggish throat centre. Physical ailments can include bronchial disease, asthma, aphonia (voice loss) and laryngitis.

As we develop as creative individuals, the increasing activity of the throat chakra draws energy up from the sacral centre providing energy for our planning of creative pursuits. Thus our appetites for food, sex and comforts are controlled but not suppressed. We learn to use money wisely in relation to the good of the whole environment and this symbolises our ability to distribute etheric energies in a healing manner.

_____CASE HISTORY _____

Marie, aged thirty-one, is a good example of how excess mental energy can react on the thyroid. She visited me with an overactive thyroid which was not responding to large amounts of the usual suppressive drug for this condition. The problem had been progressing for four years. The grey-green iris revealed heavy lymphatic toxins and weaknesses in thyroid, right kidney, and right bronchial passages. Marie's life-style was very high-powered. She was a medical sales representative, a high achiever and good at her work. She was a heavy coffee drinker and smoked twenty-five cigarettes daily. Diet included take-aways like dim sims and chips. Sleep was poor and interrupted with her thyroid condition. The Vega analysis revealed a 'biological age' of a woman in her mid-forties and the thyroid was the most stressed organ and showed as the main focus.

Marie's first month of treatment included a large daily dose of magnesium in the orotate form to stabilise the nervous system, calcium phosphate for the nervous system, Bach flower remedies to work directly on the throat chakra, homoeopathic remedies for the thyroid itself and to resolve various toxins in the system. A composite herbal tablet for sleep and relaxation included Vervain, Passiflora, and Scullcap. It should be mentioned that when choosing Bach and other flower essences and homoeopathic remedies for a particular disturbance of a chakra, the remedies are not categorised for each chakra. In terms of the Bach flowers for instance, the flowers are selected for the various emotional states that they typify and for the positive emotional states that they can produce.

On her second visit Marie reported ability to be more relaxed, a patch of improved sleeping and energy, and some skin rashes which we find often manifest as toxins are eliminated from the body. The treatment was continued with extra lymphatic drainage in the form of homoeopathic remedies. The benefits of meditation as an aid to further resolving the mental and thyroid over-activity were discussed. By the third month, Marie reported that sleep was very good, the thyroid more stabilised, smoking had been eliminated, and the 'biological age' was normal for the chronological age. The only negative point mentioned was premenstrual tension before the last period.

The remedies were repeated, with the suggestion to take more of the herbal sedative before the period. The next report was excellent, sleep, energy, well-being and relaxation were all good and meditation had been commenced. Medical drugs were now being reduced. Marie found it very helpful to read in my previous book about the connection of the throat chakra with the thyroid.

The Ajna Centre. This is the centre between the two physical eyes which is often called the third eye. In a psychological sense this centre is a further development of the sacral/throat line. It provides for the reception of the idea behind the blueprint or plan expressed through the throat centre. As the esoteric organ which synthesises the whole personality life, the ajna centre is active in all integrated persons who are ambitious in a mundane or spiritual sense. In the spiritually developed person, the ajna centre becomes an organ for distribution of spiritual energy into the environment. In the development of the average intelligent and ambitious personality, the ajna centre relates to imagination. It will tend to become activated in its lower aspect of personality ambition between the ages of twenty-one and thirty-five.

The associated endocrine gland is the pituitary and this produces hormones which stimulate all the other glands. This fact is in keeping with the concept of the ajna chakra as the synthesiser of the whole personality life. Health problems can involve the pituitary gland itself, the lower part of the brain, the eyes, ears, or sinuses and nervous system. Headaches, including migraines, are a typical expression of an imbalance involving this centre.

The ajna centre relates to that level of consciousness called the higher mind which gives us the ability for abstract thought.

It is here that we see the role of imagination which, although related to the highest level of the astral plane, performs a springboard for our conceptual or abstract thought. The ajna centre relates to the throat in its creative aspect, the solar plexus in its imaginative capacity, the heart centre in its inclusive faculty, and finally the crown centre in its potential to become an organ for distribution of spiritual energies.

_____CASE HISTORY _____

Peter, aged forty-five, had a diagnosis of vestibular neuritis which in layman's terms means a nerve inflammation involving the inner ear. Symptoms were very severe with vomiting, nausea, and extreme dizziness. He was hospitalised for one week and flat on his back in bed for another four weeks before coming to our clinic. He could only travel in the car lying down in the back of the stationwagon. The iris revealed moderately heavy lymphatic congestion, a general accumulation of acid in the tissues and nerve stress signs. Peter was a teacher and also had a large family of young children. He had felt stressed for some time. The Vega analysis indicated a raised 'biological age', stressed nervous system, sluggish liver and stress in the ajna chakra. The usual medical drug for this problem — Stemetil — was not improving the situation.

Peter was given the main mineral combination for stabilising and toning the nerves: magnesium and potassium phosphate, vitamin B-complex, the mineral combination potassium chloride and iron phosphate and selected homoeopathic remedies for the inflammation and lymphatic drainage of the ear, lymphatic draining herbs, and a homoeopathic remedy to work directly on the ajna chakra. The homoeopathic remedy Cocculus Indicus in the 30th potency was given as the specific for the dizziness and vomiting. It will be noted that once a disturbance in a chakra is manifesting through physical symptoms, the problem is dealt with from both sides of the fence, so to speak. The physical remedies provide a reflex action back towards the chakra and relieve the symptoms so that the inner stress can begin to be resolved from a psychological point of view.

On his return visit Peter reported much improvement in all

respects. Vomiting had ceased and he was out of bed and reasonably mobile. There was still some buzzing in the ears. His 'biological age' had improved according to Vega analysis and the physical disturbance from the ajna chakra was no longer registered. The remedies were repeated and on the next visit Peter reported a return to work at school which had made him very tired, but he was otherwise well. The remedies were continued and Peter and his wife then went on a trip to China during which he had good health and there was no recurrence of the ear syndrome.

The Crown Centre. This final centre corresponds to the atmic plane of spiritual will. It is found, as the name suggests, above the crown of the head and only comes into activity when all the other centres are activated and when the three etheric spinal channels are free of all impediments. At this stage of development, the crown centre becomes the final synthesis of all the other centres, major and minor, and a magnetic field is created between the ajna chakra and crown centre which draws up the Kundalini energy which is lying at the base of the spine.

The three centres above the diaphragm—head, heart and throat—are associated with the spiritual life of the individual and therefore do not automatically develop as part of the personality life. They only become active when the person takes his or her life in hand and through reflective thought, meditation and service gradually invokes those energies which can activate these centres.

The final endocrine gland to be mentioned in this area is the pineal gland which has only recently begun to yield its secrets. It is of interest that this gland has been found to be activated by light and that the crown centre is understood to become active when we can respond to spiritual light. The pineal is now acknowledged to be the master gland for the others, a role formerly attributed to the pituitary. With the base centre, the crown chakra expresses spiritual will and purpose. There is little to be said in connection with health problems of this centre except to point out the likely glandular imbalances which would result from its deficiency. An over-active state of this centre is obviously rare but occasionally, one does encounter pineal tumours. These probably result from an imbalance between the pituitary and pineal energies.

Moving back to the first premise of health as conditioned by the level on which our consciousness is focused, we can follow through the stages of human development as each level and chakra unfolds. The average person is focused at the astral or feeling level and this means most of their energies are flowing through the solar plexus centre. The astral plane will thus condition their etheric body and their physical organs. Any emotional conflict and negative emotions will have an indirect but strong effect on all bodily functions. The etheric body and health of a person conditioned by the Buddhic plane — higher counterpart of the astral plane — will be totally different. In the latter case the etheric will be conditioned by love/wisdom and by the spiritual energies flowing from the Buddhic plane.

We can contrast the above-average human state with the example of the etheric body of our domestic cat or dog. These lovable creatures are largely addicted to their appetites for food and comfort (being usually deprived of their sexual organs). The physical plane and sacral chakra is their main conditioning influence plus a developing devotion for their owners which begins to gradually develop their solar plexus chakra. They are not able to be influenced by the cosmic ethers, having no mechanism as yet for such reception.

An increasing number of individuals are becoming mentally developed and focused and they are therefore working through the throat and ajna centres and a number of health problems with nerves, head and throat, and breathing apparatus are involved. The developing love centre in humanity brings heart disturbances and a small but growing number of persons are manifesting the type of over-stimulation which comes when the centres above the diaphragm are all rapidly developing and integrating. This whole area is an immense subject of great complexity and the interested reader is urged to study the reference texts comprehensively.

CHAPTER 11

The Inherited Factors in Health and Disease

What do natural therapists mean by inherited miasms or taints? How can homoeopathy remove inherited problems? Are natural therapists talking about the same inherited problems as orthodox medicine when looking at genetic disease? Do natural therapists accept the concept of reincarnation in relation to inherited problems?

The Type of Inherited Problems Treated by Natural Therapists

Strictly speaking, many of the actual conditions which natural therapists see are understood as inherited tendencies or predispositions rather than as genetically caused conditions. In a number of cases they are problems which the orthodox profession understands as having a familial incidence. Examples are asthma, eczema, migraines, psoriasis, arthritis, circulatory problems including varicose veins, bowel and breast cancer, epilepsy, and some menstrual problems. Examples of more specific genetic disturbances are cystic fibrosis, haemophilia, and Down's syndrome.

The understanding by natural therapists of the development of the familial problems from one generation to another is of interest. The following concepts have been mainly developed by that group of natural therapists known as homoeopaths.

Having described the principles of homoeopathy, we can now look at how it is applied to inherited predispositions.

We are considering again the energy factor in health and disease. If we reduce the human body to its smallest parts we come to the sub-atomic particles called electrons. We have spoken about the etheric formative forces in Chapter 4. In the case of chronic disease patterns which appear to develop from inherited tendencies, the correct pattern has become distorted. The intepretation of miasma is a groove or fault line, and this is basically a problem which has become grafted on to the etheric body and in turn influences cells and tissues.

It is interesting that the miasms often do not manifest at the time of birth but gradually develop force and may be triggered off by outside factors. For instance, in the case of asthma there may be a similar problem in parents and grandparents but the child will be healthy for the first few years. Then after a challenge in some way to the immune system as from an immunisation, or from certain dietary articles such as dairy produce, problems develop. In the older person, grief or other emotional traumas can be a triggering factor.

Hahnemann called the inherited tendencies or predispositions miasmas and had the following to say in his famous book *The Chronic Diseases*:

> That the original malady sought for must be also of a miasmatic chronic nature clearly appeared to me. After it has once advanced and developed to a certain degree it can never be removed by the strength of any robust constitution, it can never be overcome by the most wholesome diet and order of life, nor will it die out of itself. But it is evermore aggravated from year to year through a transition into other and more serious symptoms even until the end of life.[1]

Hahnemann found that the miasms could be grouped in several broad categories. When observing patients in his practice he noted that a developing chronic disease could often be traced back to an original skin itch which had been sup-

The Main Chronic Miasms

PSORIC TAINT
Itching skin eruptions
Functional disturbances of organs
Unusual subjective sensations
The first and most primary taint

GONORRHOEAL OR SYCOTIC
Overgrowth of tissues
Warts Moles and Papillomata
Gouty concretions Osteoarthritis
Pelvic inflammations and discharges
The second or sub-acute stage

TUBERCULAR
Haemorrhages Bronchial disease
Ear and sinus infections
Enlarged lymphatic glands
Moving towards chronicity

SYPHILITIC TAINT
All distortions of body structure
Destruction of tissues such as
Ulcerations of stomach and bowel, Varicose veins and hernias
Dental caries and malocclusion
The chronic stage

pressed. He therefore gave the familial incidence group the title 'Psora' and considered this to be the oldest of all diseases:

> Psora has thus become the most infectious and general of all the chronic miasmas. For the miasm has usually been communicated to others before the one from whom it emanates has asked for or received any external repressive remedy against his itching eruption (lead water, ointment of the white precipitate of mercury,) and without confessing that he had an eruption of itch, often without knowing it himself; yea, without even the physician's or surgeon's knowing the exact nature of the eruption, which has been repressed by the lotion of lead etc.[2]

Psoric Miasm

It is of note that we find in clinical practice that the skin is the last organ to respond to treatment, thus underscoring the retracing phenomenon which was noted by Hahnemann so long ago. Natural therapists have also had repeated occasion to observe the effect of suppressing skin rashes and have noted the more serious consequences which this has on the deeper structures of the body, such as the central nervous system and respiratory system. When considering Hahnemann's ideas of contagion, we need to remind ourselves that the concept of bacteria and viruses as infective agents was unknown at that time. It is quite extraordinary that this physician was able to correctly observe the process of infectious disease with his observation of the incubation period before the skin rash.

The following conditions have been noted as related to suppressed skin rashes and therefore to the psoric miasm. Migraine and asthma are the first two examples which come to mind. This does not mean that the suppression has taken place in a single life span. The family may present with the eczema as a suppressed condition from several generations back, providing for the predisposition towards asthma and eczema in our client of today. It is in this chain of cause and effect that natural therapists will differ in their understanding of chronic disease from that of the orthodox physician. The triggering factor or allergenic substance, whether it be grass pollen, dairy products, or chemical pollutant, is only the secondary factor in the chain.

The skin manifestation itself may have a number of causes. These may be infective as in measles, German measles, or chicken pox; nervous as in nervous eczema or dermatitis; or irritant as in dermatitis caused by chemicals. The psoric miasm may also manifest as acne, but generally speaking one could say that the psoric miasm is characterised by an iching eruption on any part of the skin. In each case the body is using the skin as an excretory organ and endeavouring to eliminate toxic waste. If this function is suppressed by mercurial preparations (calomine), tar ointments, or cortisone creams what is going to happen to the toxins? They will retreat further into the system and affect the lymphatic drainage which involves a network of vessels under the skin and in connective tissue. If the lymphatic system is over-burdened then a typical problem to develop will be asthma. Hence the next generation may be born with a sluggish skin action and a predisposition towards asthma.

Apart from itching skin eruptions and the effect on lymphatic drainage from their suppression, the psoric miasm involves functional disturbances of organs without any pathology. This reminds us of the effect on the nervous system of suppressed skin rashes. It is the nervous disturbance of organs which can give an indication of psora plus the many nervous symptoms which give rise to a host of subjective sensations and symptoms. The nervous system therefore is the chief focus for many psoric ailments even if this disturbance originally started generations ago in the skin.

_____ CASE HISTORY _____

Evelyn, aged thirty-seven, attended our clinic for an itching dermatitis which covered her arms and hands. The problem had commenced four years earlier during the pregnancy with her first child. Her diet was good and the iris revealed slight lymphatic congestion, a hyper-acidity of the stomach and hypo-activity of the rest of the digestive tract. Eating eggs aggravated her condition. The fairly open structure of the iris revealed a deficiency in calcium. Vega analysis revealed that the liver and small bowel were poor in function, and the 'biological age' was moderately raised above normal.

In her first month of treatment Evelyn was given calcium phosphate, lymphatic cleansing herbs, liver toning homoeopathic drops, a mineral combination to reduce the skin inflammation, vitamin B-complex for general nerve toning, and an antidote to an environmental pollutant which was found by Vegatesting. On her return visit, Evelyn reported that the arms had improved but the hands were worse. This was not unexpected as with skin problems there is usually an inevitable initial flare as the toxins are brought to the surface. The 'biological age' had reduced which showed that overall the treatment was working. It is a valuable guide for the therapist and patient to know that they are on the right track even though the outer symptoms may seem worse.

The treatment was repeated in the second month without any obvious improvement and during the third month Evelyn suffered a miscarriage. As this caused considerable emotional stress, Bach flowers were added to a repeat of the former remedies. The liver and lymphatic remedies were changed around. It was noted by Vega evaluation that the base chakra was unbalanced and homoeopathic remedies were given for this situation which were probably related to the miscarriage. The hands began to improve at this time and then relapsed when Evelyn became pregnant again. It is a common occurrence that a pregnancy will bring a miasm to the surface and this is a good time to treat the inherited condition.

The basic remedies were continued and after another couple of months a single high potency dose of the homoeopathic remedy Arsenicum was prescribed. This remedy had previously been noted as a likely constitutional remedy for Evelyn when taking into consideration her body type, temperament, and general symptoms. Some of the pointers to this remedy from her psyche were a capacity to analyse or use the critical faculty which is often taken to excess in persons of this temperament, a tidiness about her person and a slight haughtiness. This was the turning point in the skin condition. Only three or four doses of the Arsenicum were needed at sparse intervals and Evelyn was taught to monitor when she needed another dose.

The basic vitamins, minerals and herbs were continued throughout the pregnancy which was uneventful and contrasted greatly with that of her first child. Homoeopathic Caulophyllum in the 30th potency was given to place the baby in the right position for birth as the first labour had been a problem in this respect and ended in a caesarian. A healthy baby girl was born by normal delivery. Evelyn's hands had been clear of dermatitis for many months both during and following pregnancy. Of interest in terms of the psoric miasm was the observation that not only did the skin clear but Evelyn became much more placid in temperament with her situation in life following the constitutional remedy. She may need another dose of this remedy occasionally in times of physical or emotional stress.

The Sycotic Miasm

Any health problem with recurrent catarrhal discharge from a mucous membrane is classed under the heading of Sycosis, a term coined by Hahnemann to cover this next group of disorders. It can be observed therefore that the suppressed skin disorder which became asthma with the excretion of sticky mucus in the bronchial tubes is now in this second category. The discerning reader will note that this progression is parallel with the passage of acute disease into the category we earlier named as sub-acute.

In considering the original contribution of Hahnemann to the concept of miasms, we come to an intriguing diversion. He saw this category of disease as resulting from suppressed venereal disease in the form of the gonorrhoeal infection. In deference to his genius it should be noted that homoeopaths achieve significant results by treating people suffering from the sycotic group of disorders with high potencies of the gonorrheal organism and other substances which have a similar effect on the healthy organism. We remember here the reversal effect of homoeopathic remedies. The plant Thuja is an example of a plant product related to this group of diseases and was the chief anti-sycotic remedy enunciated by Hahnemann.

Orthodox medicine may see the causal chain between treated gonorrhoea and catarrhal discharges as strange, but until 1890, 40 per cent of medical physicians practising in the USA were homoeopaths who accepted this concept. Needless to say, a person who inherits this miasm does not develop gonorrhoea in the infectious sense. This has not prevented some over-cautious health departments from making the use of homoeopathic nosodes illegal. (Nosodes is the technical term given to a substance made from a disease-producing substance.) As there are no physical molecules present after the 25th potency this attitude is patently illogical. The absence of physical molecules in these remedies does give assurance to the public that no harm can come from a homoeopath who uses nosodes.

There are other disorders in this group apart from catarrhal discharges and these include problems with infected ears, sinuses, teeth, bronchial tubes, the vagina or bowel. Polyps, warts, fibroids and all benign tumours are grouped under this miasm. Gouty concretions and adhesions also feature strongly and include, therefore, the rheumatic and osteo-arthritic disorders. Some writers have characterised this group of disorders as featuring an overgrowth of tissue. It is true that many people in this category tend to be generally overweight and can suffer from retention of fluid. This is sometimes also described as the hydrogenoid constitution, from the tendency to accumulate fluid.

The ever-increasing incidence of pelvic inflammatory disease is understood by homoeopaths to be directly related to the increasing incidence of this miasm. At this point of the story an attempt should be made to relate the subjective factors in Chapter 10 to the miasms. A disturbance in the sacral chakra was described as relating to pelvic disease connected to the reproductive organs.

On the one hand, therefore, we have the miasmatic tendency which is inherited from forebears who suffered from the active form of gonorrhoea, and we have perhaps in the present situation various triggering factors. These may be suppression of skin manifestations as the body endeavours to eliminate toxins, life-style factors such as poor diet, stress and environmental toxins. More specifically in terms of this miasm, sexual promiscuity appears to be a triggering factor in pelvic inflammatory disease. The reader may consider this merely results from the infective factor. The natural therapist finds however that pelvic inflammatory problems, venereal warts, venereal herpes, and cervical dysplasia will be more common and persistent in those who would be classified as having the sycotic miasm. AIDS will be discussed under the syphilitic miasm.

From a subjective point of view, resolution of the problem will need to be made in terms of a balance of energy in the sacral chakra. This may be viewed as the prime causative factor in the chain of disturbances which lead to the miasm. This concept is in line with that of the etheric formative forces as basic to health and disease. The homoeopath does not necessarily need to subscribe to these subjective factors to achieve a cure because the correct homoeopathic remedy will, through its energetic effect, work into the disturbance of the etheric. If the psychology of the client is markedly disturbed in terms of chakra balance and function, the condition will tend to recur in spite of correct homoeopathic treatment and may be a reason for therapy-resistant patients. The life-style and emotional factors of the case should therefore be taken into consideration.

_____ CASE HISTORY _____

Jasmine, aged thirty-six, came for naturopathic treatment for abnormal cells of the cervix which were found by a smear test. She had a history of surgery for fibroids and a lot of pelvic adhesions were found. These conditions are all common under the heading of this particular miasm. Before being referred to me by another naturopath she had lymphatic herbs for cleansing, homoepathic liver drops, silica tablets for the adhesion tendency, and the mineral salt potassium chloride to assist the herbs to cleanse the lymphatic system.

On her first visit to me the 'biological age' was found to be in the pre-malignancy range and the cervix and uterus were the organ which cross-checked with the highest 'biological age'. Secondary tissues and organs associated with the problem involved the lymphatic system and vagina. I decided that if there was no improvement by the next visit, that surgery would have to be recommended. The miasmatic remedy given for the condition was Medorrhinum in the 30th potency. This is the nosode for the gonorrheal miasm but it was chosen from amongst other possible remedies and the potency and dose had to be carefully evaluated. In this case, two drops were given twice daily and it was expected that the remedy would be needed over several months. Vitamins A and C were added to the other basic remedies as a general means for improving the health of the epithelial tissue of cervix, uterus and vagina.

On her next visit the 'biological age' was found to be moving towards normal and this improvement continued, over the next few months. The remedies were all continued with the addition of homoeopathic Ipecachuana for nausea which was a new symptom. Jasmine is now feeling very well in herself and during a recent long trip to India had no health problems although many of her fellow-travellers did. She will shortly have another smear test to check on her progress medically. It is of note that Jasmine's psychological outlook and attitudes are very positive and this seems to indicate that the inherited condition is likely to be resolved for good.

In terms of treatment it can be very helpful to understand this concept of inherited predisposition. A skilled therapist can see from a simple observation of body type what miasm is likely to manifest and therefore know what group of remedies to consider. A patient is often therapy-resistant until the underlying miasm is treated. It is generally found best to treat the miasms only when they are actively manifesting some of their symptoms. Thus, a psoric remedy will be chosen when an itching skin rash or nervous problem is uppermost and a remedy from the sycotic group when a catarrhal discharge, wart or fibroid manifests.

The Tubercular Miasm

In the development of homoeopathy, initially the tubercular taint was not considered as a separate miasm but as a combination of the two previous miasms. These days it is more practical and meaningful to regard the tubercular miasm as a separate entity. As with the other miasms the original process often occurred many generations ago with infection from the actual tubercular bacillus. This manifests in later generations as a bronchial weakness in some members of the family tree. We have observed in many cases a lesion showing in the bronchial section of the iris. Sometimes this manifests actively as asthma and in other cases remains quite dormant. On questioning families with such lesions, they are sometimes aware of tuberculosis earlier in the family.

Other manifestations involving this problem are recurrent sinus problems, ear infections in children, enlarged lymph nodes in neck, groin and axilla, and the tendency to purulent yellow/green secretions from mucous membranes. A recurrent tendency to nosebleeds is nearly always a sure sign of this miasm. The shape of the body can be very typical in a tubercular type. The chest may be narrow and hollow and the posture inclined to be stooped. In some cases, the chest will be hollow or flat but the abdomen bloated and saucer-shaped.

As with the other miasms, we are not considering a condition which will ever manifest active tuberculosis. The natural therapist will give a tubercular nosode at some stage in the treatment and this can produce very good results in persistent asthma cases. It is particularly useful to resolve this problem in childhood so that bronchial conditions are cleared up before they become chronic. We have observed that the tubercular taint prevents the correct assimilation of calcium in children and this may partly account for their underdevelopment and for the bronchial weakness.

In terms of the progression from acute to chronic disease, the tubercular taint tends to come late in the sub-acute stage as it moves towards chronic disease. This is in keeping with the purulent discharges and the tubercular 'caverns' which take place in the untreated chest of the active infectious disease.

In considering the subjective aspects associated with the tubercular taint, it is in one sense a reversal to the sycotic miasm where overgrowth and over-activity of the sacral centre manifest. The tubercular state results from deprivation in various ways. At the physical level we have lack of sunlight and hence the improvement which was noted in patients in sanatoria in sunny climates. The inability to respond and process light in an inner sense has been noted by anthroposophical doctors.[3] This could be interpreted as the need to take in more spiritual energy. In *Esoteric Healing* by Bailey, the tubercular person is understood to have imposed a kind of emotional starvation on themselves.[4] The solar plexus chakra is therefore involved and is not open to a free flow of energy. It is of interest that in the previous century writers often suffered from tuberculosis. This would involve possible over-activity or imbalance of the throat chakra and perhaps a depletion in the solar plexus centre at the same time.

_____ CASE HISTORY _____

Bianca, aged fifty-six, had a history of sinusitis and asthma. The lymphatic congestion in her system was obvious from the iris and the sympathetic nervous system was in a state of imbalance. She had suffered breathing problems for four years. Other problems included fluid retention in the legs and rheumatism in the shoulders. The 'biological age' was raised according to Vega analysis and the lymphatic system featured as the prime cause of the problem. The causal chain was the lymphatic system, then bronchial passages, then sinus. In this case there were two miasmatic influences associated with the asthma—the sycotic (gonorrheal taint) and the tubercular. The rheumatism, fluid retention and sinus revealed the first, and also her general body shape which is fairly stocky. The lymphatic congestion was related to both miasms and the asthma to the tubercular taint.

The first month of treatment included a number of remedies to resolve the lymphatic congestion—vitamin C, a mineral combination of iron phosphate and potassium chloride, lymphatic herbs in solid extract and homoeopathic form, and a mineral combination of calcium phosphate and sodium phosphate to strengthen the bronchial area. The gonorrheal nosode Medorrhinum was administered in the M potency at weekly intervals for four doses. On her second visit there was no improvement and the remedies were repeated except for the nosode. It was replaced by the tubercular nosode Tuberculinum which was given in the 200th potency twice weekly. On the third visit, there was still no improvement with the asthma although the 'biological age' had reduced so I knew the remedies were working.

On the fourth visit she reported that the shoulder had improved but the asthma was still a problem and a lot of mucus was experienced in the throat. It should be mentioned that her husband was a heavy smoker and the smoke was found to aggravate her asthma and sinus. The remedies were repeated with the addition of a large herbal mixture for the chest which included Lobelia, Marshmallow, Liquorice, Coltsfoot, Horehound and Trifolium.

On the fifth visit, two months later, she reported the first real improvement in the asthma. She continued to make steady progress from this point onwards and has not needed to visit the clinic for some time. Her daughter, however, reports periodically on her progress and was perhaps the most encouraging influence, persuading her to persevere with the treatment for a number of months in spite of little initial response. This is a good case to illustrate the necessity of patience with the treatment process, especially when there is more than one miasm involved.

The Syphilitic Miasm

In the discussion from acute to chronic disease the model used explained how the suppression of toxins eventually involves destructive tissue changes. In the syphilitic group of miasmatic disorders we have an inherited predisposition towards perversion of structure. Once again, there will be no revival or expectation of active infectious syphilis on the part of the client. The following minor and large problems may be included in this group—malocclusion of teeth (crooked teeth), varicose veins, aneurisms (ruptured blood vessels), ulcers of skin or mucous membrane in mouth, stomach or bowel, rickets and other bony abnormalities, rheumatoid arthritis, AIDS and all auto-immune disorders.

We now come to a sobering consideration. Chronic disease in all communities is increasing. This includes arthritis, cancer, circulatory disorders and recently, the horrifying increase of AIDS—the ultimate in destructive processes. It is interesting to trace AIDS in terms of the syphilitic miasm as so much of its progress is typical. First there is the initial spread which appears to have been accelerated by excessive promiscuity. Then there is the slow development of destructive processes within the T-lymphocytes of the blood which involves immune function; there is the subsequent vulnerability to other destructive disease processes such as cancer, and the total emaciation of the body in the AIDS sufferer which is so typical of the syphilitic miasm.

The concept of Hahnemann in relation to the syphilitic miasm would be unacceptable to modern medical scientists. He claimed that if the original external manifestation of the disease in the form of the chancre or small ulcer was left untouched, the internal manifestation into secondary and tertiary syphilis would not take place. In practice this means that the chancre should be treated homoeopathically before it has time to manifest internally.

Subjectively speaking, the venereal taint of syphilis will also be connected with misuse of energy through the sacral centre. At this point the question may be asked, what about those individuals who contract infective pelvic disease through only one sexual contact or who contract AIDS through a blood transfusion? How does this relate to their sacral centre which may not be subject to misuse of energy in any way?

A diversion will be made here to consider how the theory of reincarnation may be connected to the manifestation of chronic and destructive disease patterns which do not seem to be related to the actions of their sufferer.

Reincarnation and Inherited Disease

In Chapter 9 perfect health was discussed in terms of a free flow of energy to every part of our being. Any blocks at either psychological, etheric or physical levels can cut off our health-bringing energies. In the first analysis, health flows from our inner essence or soul, that intangible bestower of beauty, insight and wisdom which has been given many names in different religions but which is always understood as that part of us which is divine.

From Eastern philosophy, the teaching about the mechanism of soul consciousness has been preserved and transmitted into the West by particular teachers who have made this tradition intelligible to Western man.[5] People have, however, become confused by the teaching about reincarnation both from Eastern and Western sources. Many people imagine that reincarnation involves the arbitrary birth of our soul into animal, vegetable or human forms according to luck or misdemeanours. The taking of an animal form by a human is transmigration and has nothing to do with the normal process of reincarnation.

The process of reincarnation involves the gradual perfection of soul expression through a personality involving many hundreds of lifetimes. The process is governed by the soul attracting during each incarnation those personality vehicles through which it can best express itself at any particular stage of development. The physical/etheric, astral (emotional), and mental vehicles will be conditioned in each life by the previous experiences and this largely governs the health, development and interests of any individual following birth.

As a person grows and develops, their present state can be modified considerably by their attitudes and life-style and previous limitations can be offset. We could compare this with the law of gravity in the physical world which mankind has learnt to overcome so that the use of flying machines for communication is quite effortless. Thus the law of karma which is so glibly discussed by the average person who has dipped briefly into Eastern religious thought is not usually correctly understood. It is true that misuse of our personality vehicles may be the cause of health problems in our present life, but we should not take the view that this suffering and limitation needs to continue until death. The creative use of meditation and of natural therapies can change many persons predisposed to illness into magnetic and healthy individuals.

When considering the case of an innocent person who is suddenly struck by an unfortunate illness we need to consider both the inner and outer causes. There may have been a slumbering miasm which has been triggered off or brought to the surface by an outer cause, such as an infection like AIDS through blood transfusion following an accident. Disease is often the coming together of the inner and outer causes. The inner cause may have been set in motion by the individual many lives ago and the present disease is the final working out of that problem. In such a case death is often the best release for the soul and is only seen as a disaster from our limited vision. The frantic efforts of modern medicine to preserve life at any cost, even to the maintaining of a life completely devoid of quality, is a reflection of our materialistic attitude in the twentieth century.

Through the increasing personal experience of soul consciousness on the part of many individuals, the whole subject of dying, death and reincarnation will take on new meaning. The recording and teaching about near-death experiences (NDEs), out-of-the-body experiences (OBs) plus the increasing testimonies of meditation experiences is the first stage in our new understanding. Both euthanasia and *in vitro* fertilisation debates will be seen in a totally different light when it is accepted that the soul is an immortal entity which ever grows from life to life. It is interesting that the general change in attitudes is taking place as the result of direct experiences on the part of many individuals and not as a result of book learning from either East or West. Nevertheless, the infiltration of Eastern concepts has provided for the mental expansion and understanding of different levels of consciousness as they are now being experienced on a wide scale by humanity.

The actual mechanism of reincarnation as taught by the Trans-Himalayan school is that when a soul is ready to incarnate, the mental vehicle is the first to develop.[6] The substance of the mental plane which is appropriate for the particular stage of mental development of the individual concerned will be automatically attracted. This will be quite different, for instance, in the case of a soul who has developed artistic or mathematical abilities from a soul who has previously been largely concerned with physical survival in terms of eating, gathering food and copulating. When the mental substance has been organised a note is struck by the reincarnating soul at astral levels and the process repeated in astral substance. The mental and astral levels are quite apart from any influence of the future parents, although there may be a karmic correspondence provided by the parents which will give the environment for the indwelling mental and astral qualities to manifest.

The etheric level is organised just before fertilisation on the physical plane by the future parents. It is at this point that the genetic constitution may carry the miasmatic seeds for disease from the physical bodies of the parents. The fact that children within a family have different genetic constitutions relates to the conditioning factors previously mentioned. There is a choice by the soul which is conditioned by karmic factors and which the soul on its own plane fully understands is providing the right environment and opportunities for its future growth and experience. The etheric/physical, astral and mental vehicles provide for the mechanism commonly called the personality. They are the levels of consciousness around which the reincarnating soul cycles continuously until perfection is achieved in a particular life.

At the close of each life, the outer form is the first to die and the etheric body disintegrates after a few days, or more quickly in the case of cremation. The indwelling consciousness is gradually released back towards the soul. The individual spends from months to many years on the astral levels following death according to their interests and needs. This accounts for some of the mediumistic activities which can take place with the living. At some stage the soul withdraws the consciousness on to the mental level and once again the time span variation here is large depending on the soul development. This is the traditional heaven world of orthodox religions and provides for a blissful state in the case of the average person. Wide awake souls who are concerned to continue their active service as soon as possible at the physical level will forego any long stay at this level and will prepare themselves to cycle down into incarnation again.

The reincarnation process provides for rational explanation of the great variations in health, qualities and attributes which we find within humanity. The concept tends to appeal to those persons who find orthodox religions as usually presented to be lacking in a reasonable explanation for the suffering and misery of large sections of mankind. Such thinking persons are unwilling to be placated by the promises of a better life in the next world provided we meekly accept our suffering. Of necessity, this description of the reincarnation process has been simplified and abbreviated and the interested reader is advised to study the subject from a number of angles.

Application of Homoeopathy to Genetic Factors

The process of homoeopathic potentisation has been previously described as having the ability to change sub-atomic and etheric structure. It is the one natural therapy which can help people to alter genetic endowment once they have taken the right psychological attitude which will transmute the basic underlying causes for ill health on the inner planes of feeling and thought. The approach which Hahnemann developed has been further developed and refined by a school of medical homoeopaths and constitutional prescribing has resulted.

The constitutional remedy covers both genetic inheritance and temperament of the client. The temperament will cover those feeling and thinking attributes which have been engendered partly by the inherited factors and partly by the physical and psychic environment of the individual. Modern homoeopaths tend to distinguish between the constitutional remedy and the use of intercurrent remedies which may be given for the particular inherited miasms of the person. The client may also need different remedies for acute conditions as they arise during a healing crisis. Many constitutional remedies do cover the particular miasms of the person, but at certain times an extra boost is needed to eradicate a particular malady and so a specific nosode will be prescribed.[7]

It has been my experience over many years that homoeopathy works much better after an initial period of cleansing with herbs and biochemical balancing with minerals and the water-soluble vitamins of B-complex and C. During treatment with constitutional remedies, nosodes, herbs and homoeopathic mixtures involving low potencies, homoeopathic remedies to stimulate elimination and organ drainage are also included. This prevents any accumulation of toxins in the blood which might give unpleasant symptoms during the healing phase.

The following case is a good example to round off and illustrate the constitutional factors mentioned in homoeopathic prescribing. The constitutional remedy will often cover the miasmatic problem and in the case of the remedy Lycopodium used here, we have a polychrest. This is a remedy which can cover all the miasms in a person who corresponds to its pattern.

CASE HISTORY

Cyrano first visited me a number of years ago for a rheumatic condition. His brown iris is of fine texture and is marked by radii solaris which are radial dark spokes often associated with accumulation of toxic waste in the gastrointestinal area. He described himself as having a very critical temperament and was indeed a very articulate and perceptive client. After a few months on liver, lymphatic and rheumatic herbs, a mineral combination for inflammation of the joints and vitamins B and C, the rheumatic condition was much improved.

During this first period of basic treatment, the underlying miasmatic condition became illustrated on the skin by the sudden appearance on the forehead of a small growth which looked like a combination of a wart and mole. I had already decided that the constitutional remedy was Lycopodium according to the temperament of the client. One dose in the 10M potency was needed and within the month the mole, which was about 8mm and very raised, totally disappeared. There was a further improvement in the rheumatic condition which is a common one in Lycopodium subjects. In case the reader should imagine that this is a remedy to be prescribed for all moles and rheumatism I should say that in seventeen years with about 10 000 clients I have only found it to be indicated in about five cases!

The Lycopodium person has a very rational type of mind and yet they are also at the same time governed by their emotions. They are often leaders at home or in the work sphere and can sometimes be experienced as dictatorial in attitude. I have found this remedy to be sometimes suited to very articulate persons who do not suffer fools gladly. One particular lady who responded very well with this remedy always sat in my chair when sent into the consulting room ahead of me.

In keeping with his temperament, Cyrano was not interested in keeping on with the remedies any longer than absolutely necessary. They were therefore tapered off and he was not seen for a couple of years until returning with his wife who was in an advanced stage of cancer. She was too far progressed with her disease for natural therapies to have any significant effect although an attempt was made to help. At this time, Cyrano was given basic nerve treatment and one more dose of Lycopodium as he was very irritable and stressed by the situation.

He returned some time after the death of his wife in a fairly depressed state and reported that life had lost its meaning over the last nine months. His rheumatism had returned and the 'biological age' was moderately raised. Some time was spent talking about the meaning of life and death and of losing a loved one and of the need for new interests to be found. It is rarely sufficient to just give a pile of remedies during such times of psychological adjustment.

The remedies for this recurrence of arthritis included the mineral salt sodium phosphate for acid deposits in the tissue, rheumatic and liver herbs, potassium and magnesium phosphate and vitamin B-complex for general nerve energy and toning, and another dose of the constitutional remedy Lycopodium in the 10M potency. At the next visit Cyrano reported he was much better especially after three weeks. He reported having begun to entertain again. The 'biological age' had improved. At the next visit he reported being well in himself but the arthritis after the initial improvement was stationary. It was suggested that the deadly nightshade family, which includes tomatoes, potatoes and peppers, be excluded from the diet. By the next visit the arthritis was 80–90 per cent improved but he had suffered a very bad sore throat for three weeks. The treatment was adjusted for this factor. He then went away for three weeks and forgot to take his remedies and the arthritis relapsed a little. The basic remedies were continued for another few months and one more dose of the constitutional remedy was given with further good results for the arthritis and for an acid dyspeptic condition. The remedies were then tapered off.

I find it difficult to imagine my naturopathic practice without these very selective homoeopathic aids for treating inherited predispositions. It is true that a number of cases respond very well to vitamins, minerals and herbs in a few months and they appear to need no further treatment for some months and even years. Every therapist is confronted with many cases which provide more of a challenge in terms of their family background, constitution and environment. To be able to influence health in a positive sense in such cases is to be truly creative. This recreation of the life of another person is very satisfying and rewarding.

Having moved into the sphere of psychology with a description of constitutional homoeopathic prescribing, the next chapter addresses how natural therapies may influence or relate to the psychology of the client.

CHAPTER 12

Psychology and Natural Therapies

Are natural therapists qualified to use psychology in practice? How do natural therapies work with psychological conditions? What are the psychological conditions which natural therapists can help? How do the esoteric or subjective aspects already discussed fit in with psychological conditions commonly met in practice?

Natural therapists do not usually undertake extensive training in psychology. Within the naturopathic courses accredited by the Australian Natural Therapists Association there is an essential component of behavioural sciences. This is to enable graduates to understand normal psychological growth and to recognise basic problems so that they can refer clients to appropriately trained persons. There are also compulsory courses in counselling skills in the accredited courses, plus training in human relations.

Physicians of all kinds constantly need these skills whether in orthodox medicine or the many complimentary groups. There is never a day in the consulting room without some need for using skills and understanding how to deal with the psychosomatic aspects of health disorders. The perceptive physician is able to recognise when a physical ailment has a psychological undercurrent whether it is indigestion, insomnia, exhaustion, dermatitis, or arthritis. Perhaps one of the most needed perceptions in health work is to be able to give suitable 'weighting' to the physical and psychomatic factors in any illness or disorder.

I have developed a basic guideline or model in this area over a number of years in this consulting work. It goes something like this. After taking a careful case history I make my physical assessment using Vega analysis, iris diagnosis, palpation and any other physical aids which seem indicated. Already, there is a good indication of the extent of the physical problem and its acuteness, severity or chronicity. I balance these factors against the experience of the client. Sometimes there is a big discrepancy.

For instance, take the cases of allergies which now plague natural therapists. Very often there is nothing in the iris or Vega analysis to indicate the extreme discomfort suffered by some people. Not all persons with exhaustion, abdominal bloating, flatulence, diarrhoea or constipation fall into the category of neurotic but an increasing number do unfortunately. As discussed in Chapter 10, we find that an imbalance or conflict at the feeling or astral level will result in a disturbed solar plexus energy centre and this will, in turn, disrupt all the digestive activities. Modern trends have encouraged these persons to view their problem as coming from outside factors in the form of foods which they cannot handle.

In any psychosomatic disorder there is an overlap between the physical and psychological factors. Due to our modern Western life-style and poor eating habits, the digestive enzymes often become severely impaired and it is certainly true that in such a state allergies will manifest easily. It is interesting, however, that some persons with these problems make significant recovery with a few months' treatment (see Chapter 7) and others appear to be therapy-resistant patients. The latter group tend to move from one therapist to another over many months of treatment, bringing their lists of foods, or in some cases, endless samples of foods to be examined for compatibility. These persons have become fixated on their problems and have thus increased the physical irritation by their constant attention to every gurgle or movement in the digestive system.

There is no doubting the genuine pain of the sufferer but it is a pertinent axiom that energy follows thought. The illustration of allergies has been used because it is very widespread in the community. Other typical examples relate to the fear and anxieties of the therapy-resistant asthma patient, or the partially externalised stress of persons suffering from a variety of inflammatory skin ailments.

Having estimated the relative proportions of physical and psychological parameters of any disorder, I first deal with the physical side for several months to see how much improvement can take place. Where there is a minimum of emotional conflict, the patient usually always shows considerable improvement within two months and this is consolidated in the next two months. Remedies are tapered off between five and nine months depending on the severity of the situation. The therapy-resistant patient often makes no improvement in the first three months. Having investigated the possibility of the underlying miasmatic predispositions, of geopathic stress or environmental toxins, it is then time to investigate the feelings and thoughts of the patient more fully.

Almost without fail, an underlying psychological problem surfaces. It would have been inappropriate to discuss this on the first two or three visits. This type of patient has already tried to blame the problem on physical causes which they hope are amenable to natural therapies. Sometimes they make minimal improvement but can go no further. I find that the person is then ready to admit the possibility of the cause being emotional. Very often it will be a problem in the family life, at work, or poor life-style in terms of spacing work, study, relaxation and family duties. There will often be a problem of human relationships which it is very helpful for the therapist to articulate more fully with the patient.

In such instances there is often no need in the case of the natural therapist to refer the patient to a psychologist or psychiatrist. For therapists who do not feel adequate in this area of counselling, there are a number of good community counselling services available through local councils. The client can therefore continue to attend the natural therapist for the physical remedies and perhaps go once a week for counselling at the same time. It will be found that the physical remedies will work much better. Having explored the situation to some extent, the therapist is able to be more specific in prescribing suitable homoeopathic remedies or flower essences for the particular emotional states.

Remedies Which Influence Psychosomatic Problems

There are specific physical remedies which can help psychological states. In the area of vitamins, the B-complex group is the main item to consider in terms of nervous stress which often results from psychological problems. B1 is useful for depression and energy and for poor appetite, B3 is valuable for its biochemical effect in insomnia, hallucinations and several psychiatric conditions, B5 for extreme exhaustion and B6 for pre-menstrual tension. Unless there is a severe problem such as hallucinations or sensory disturbances of the schizophrenias, it is usually best to give a B-complex which covers all the group. In particular problems a B-complex can accompany the specific B component which is specific for the ailment. Vitamin C is the other water-soluble stress vitamin and is also very basic for cases of physical, psychological or nervous stress. The other vitamins are not specific for this area.

Due to the excessive public awareness and concern with vitamins, the basic mineral salts needed for the nervous system are often overlooked. A lot of time and energy can be wasted on vitamins and the basic building blocks of healthy nerve function ignored. The two salts most needed are potassium phosphate and magnesium phosphate.[1] The potassium phosphate is needed for transmission of nerve energy and is given in all cases of exhaustion, lack of concentration and poor memory, and is considered as the main mineral food for the grey matter of the brain and nervous system. The magnesium phosphate is essential wherever there is excess tension as in nervous spasm, tics, insomnia, tension headaches and for stress in any part of the body. Zinc is another mineral which has sedating properties, and in the presence of a deficiency a person can become excessively fidgety. This deficiency is often observed in the compulsive foot-tapping of adolescent boys.

As these all seem to be nervous parameters rather than psychological states, how does one apply these remedies for what seem to be psychological problems? A person who comes to the clinic with anxieties, fears or insomnia will often have some of these nervous symptoms such as exhaustion, lack of concentration, and tension headaches. In other words there is a crossover between the emotional problems and the nervous manifestations. By giving the physical remedies first for a few months, the extent of psychological component becomes more obvious.

Another consideration surfaces here. If a person has a long period of psychological stress, they use up particular vitamins and minerals more easily than under normal conditions. It seems a logical conclusion that the endless firing of their nerve cells will deplete the system of potassium phosphate. Vitamin B as a water-soluble vitamin is easily used up with stress.[2] After these deficiencies have become marked and the biochemistry disturbed, it is very easy to slip into a depressive state which really has a physical basis. Unless the deficiencies are corrected, very real psychological states can become grafted onto the original physical depression. A vicious circle is thus created and the deadening effect of modern drugs does little to help the problem.

There are a number of herbs which are useful in conjunction with vitamin B-complex. These are mainly the traditional relaxing herbs like Scullcap, Valerian, Passiflora, Vervain and Motherwort. They can be helpful for tensions of many kinds and no doubt contain the minerals already mentioned. Hops, Gentian and Avena Sativa are herbs which have an energising and toning effect on the nervous system. These are often blended with the more sedative herbs to give an all-round nerve tonic. None of these herbs are habit forming or addictive.

All the remedies discussed so far have a physical basis for their prescribing but the flower essence remedies are in a class all by themselves and are specifically prescribed for a wide range of emotional states. These essences were originally pioneered by Edward Bach, a Harley Street physician who gave up standard medical practice to search for remedies in the English countryside which would help the more causative factors which he encountered in his clients. Thirty-eight flowers were selected for various problems and these were tested by Bach himself after his sensitivity caused him to take on the condition of the patient.[3] Examples of these flower essences are Larch for lack of confidence, Cherry Plum for feelings of desperation, Star of Bethlehem for shock, Gorse for hopelessness and despair, and Scleranthus for indecision.

The flowers are picked when the sun is at its meridian and are soaked for several hours in water from an unpolluted stream. The solution is then filtered to remove the flowers and the essence preserved with brandy. It will be observed that the solution could not contain much in the way of physical molecules of the plant and they therefore can be considered as having a homoeopathic effect. Bach did his work in the 1920s and 1930s and over the last ten years, a number of flowers have been added to the repertory. This later research has taken place mainly in Colorado and California in the USA and in Queensland, Australia.

When prescribing the flower essences, it is usual for the therapist to select about five essences according to the emotional states of the client as perceived by the therapist. This provides another good reason for the therapist to become aware through observation and dialogue of the psychology of the client. The more articulate clients can assist the therapist greatly by expressing how they react to life and particular situations, and the self-aware client is almost able to select their own flower essences. It is of interest that clients become very aware of the effect of the flower essences even if they have not been told that they have been prescribed for balancing emotional states. They will make comments to the effect that they are happier or more calm on the prescribed Bach drops.

Although it may seem that the flower essences are influencing the emotions from outside, it has been noticed that not everyone can respond to this therapy. There still has to be that basic move towards wholeness on the part of the client which seems to open the door for any therapy to work fully. Some people will say that the effect is therefore all placebo. The placebo effect does not seem to account for the amazing effect of the Bach flowers on cats, dogs and horses.

_____CASE HISTORY_____

There was a recent call from a woman in a country area who shows dogs. One of her dogs had a particular temperamental quirk which was driving her to distraction. It involved extreme irritability, impatience and anxiety. She was advised to collect the Bach flowers called Impatiens, Mimulus, Cherry Plum, Star of Bethlehem and Rock Rose plus magnesium phosphate and administer them in solution to the dog. Three weeks later she rang to say the dog was completely transformed in temperament.

It is understood and experienced now that the flower essences affect consciousness via the energy centres or chakras and that they have a direct effect on the etheric realm which is the bridge between psychological states and the physical body. The essences appear to have a reflex action from the etheric into the emotional and mental worlds of the person. They possibly set up a resonance based on a particular harmonic frequency. It has been postulated that the flower is the most spiritualised portion of the plant and that is why the essence from a flower can have such a far-reaching effect on the human psyche. One theory suggests that the crystalline structures which have been demonstrated as existing in the blood, bones and nervous system can store and amplify the vibrational and harmonic effects from homoeopathic remedies and flower essences.

The actual mechanism by which either traditional homoeopathic remedies or flower essences can affect feelings and thoughts is yet to be fully delineated. One finding in clinical practice is obvious. The clients who are able to take a more positive direction for growth and creativity are those who do both the psychological work and take suitable remedies. The remedies appear to remove the etheric blocks so that psychological and spiritual energies can flow through to the physical brain consciousness and nervous system. In psychosomatic disorders, because of the overlap of psychological and physical disturbances, it is impossible to say which area changes first or whether the process takes place all in one. It does seem to me that having observed the long time people normally take to change in counselling or therapy programmes, a combination of psychological work and natural therapies has an immense advantage in terms of quick results.

It is often appropriate to commence the treatment with physical remedies.

CASE HISTORIES

The case of Lorraine, a thirty-two-year-old bank clerk, was typical. She attended the clinic after having been on very heavy medication for depression for eight years. She was also a heavy drinker and consumed ten glasses of wine daily after work. Her face had the typical mask-like appearance of the heavily sedated person. There were symptoms of backache and neckache; all symptoms were worse before the menstrual period. She was, of course, in a state of exhaustion and nerve depletion in spite of the fact that by iris diagnosis the basic constitution was good and under normal circumstances would require little supplementation. The Vega analysis revealed a raised 'biological age' and the liver was stressed from the pharmaceutical medication and alcohol.

The first month of treatment consisted of a combination capsule containing vitamin B-complex, potassium, magnesium and calcium phosphate and small amounts of other substances such as zinc. For dealing with the liver sluggishness a herbal tablet was given containing the liver herbs Dandelion, Wahoo, Fringe Tree and St Mary's Thistle. The Bach flowers Mustard, Gorse, Walnut, Rockrose and Cherry Plum were used whenever she felt emotionally disturbed. In addition, rheumatic herbs for a skeletal condition and homoeopathic medication for the thyroid were included.

Great improvement took place during the first month. She came back with a totally different expression on the face, mobile but relaxed, was off all drugs and had almost given up her heavy coffee drinking but was still consuming the same quantity of wine. Energy was much improved and the Vega analysis indicated a lower 'biological age' plus improvement to liver function. The remedies were continued and Lorraine was advised to take the Bach remedies more often to help the drinking problem. At the next visit she reported reducing the wine to three glasses and had lost 3·5 kg.

At the next visit Lorraine reported continued general improvement but explained she still felt bad before and during the menstrual period. She had also started to eat more and had slipped back into her drinking pattern. An extra homoeopathic mixture was given for the menstrual stress and the other remedies continued with minor changes. It became obvious by the sixth visit that more than the physical remedies were needed as she suffered a bad relapse with the drinking. It was then that it seemed valuable to explore the psychological undercurrents to her health disturbance. She explained that she did not like going home after work because her three children and shift-worker husband got the place into such a mess. There was concern that the standard of cleanliness taught to her was not able to be maintained.

It was suggested that the Bach remedies be used more frequently, especially before going home and on arriving home. It was also recognised that new attitudes to the house problem would have to be adopted, for instance viewing it as a temporary problem which would pass as the children got older and making the decision to clean the house only once a week no matter how dirty it became. Lorraine pointed out that other people might see it in a mess but on questioning she admitted that hardly anybody visited unannounced. We also discussed the relevance of a dirty house versus a sick body if she kept drinking.

On the next visit Lorraine reported that she had made an effort to cope with the existing situation by using her flower essences more often and taking a more philosophical approach to life. To her amazement, the children and husband appeared to respond to her new attitude by becoming much more tidy and helpful.

The case of Shirley is another typical one where a blend of discussion and remedies appeared to work wonders. Shirley attended the clinic intermittently during her middle age for a variety of subclinical disorders. She was greatly overweight and suffered periods of exhaustion and at one stage a very severe respiratory infection which finally resulted in cracked ribs from coughing. Perhaps we should have realised her propensity for calcium imbalance at this stage.

Some months then went by before she returned following a fractured humerus bone in the upper arm which refused to heal. In spite of every natural aid which could be summoned in the way of vitamins, herbs, minerals and homoeopathic remedies, the bone refused to heal. She even followed the treatment of a veterinarian who had a brilliant reputation for treating stubborn fractures in horses. I also suggested she attend a medical doctor who specialised in the healing of fractures through the use of magnetic currents. The orthodox treatment was six surgical operations which she refused. She continued with basic natural remedies to keep her general health in as much order as possible and resigned herself to putting up with the pain in her arm and an ever-increasing lump around the fracture site, which I presume was a conglomerate of improper calcification and scar tissue.

Some time later she returned again for further assessment and explained that she felt very emotionally disturbed and at the end of her tether. The family were getting her down, and she felt she had no personal space since her husband had retired and the married children always needed her help and counsel. I suggested we include the husband in the discussion and asked if he felt that he could get his own breakfast and lunch to leave Shirley more free to follow her own pursuits. He readily agreed. As Shirley was already taking basic herbs, minerals and vitamins, I gave her only Natrum Sulphuricum in the 200th potency which is probably her constitutional; magnesium phosphate in the 30th potency for chest pain; and the Bach flowers: Hornbeam, Mimulus and White Chestnut.

Following her departure, Shirley's daughter phoned and was very concerned about the health of her mother. I received an entirely different account — from the daughter's point of view she was constantly summoned to help her mother. It is not really the job of the therapist to make judgements about who is right in such a situation so I suggested to Shirley's daughter that she only visit her mother once a month so that Shirley would then have space to develop her own life.

A couple of months later, Shirley returned for a check-up in a very positive frame of mind and was convinced that the Bach remedies had done wonders to improve her attitudes. I explained that the constitutional homoeopathic remedy would also have helped and it became obvious that the family situation was much improved, Shirley explained that now she felt able to get on with her life. It is very difficult to judge what emphasis to place on the remedies and what to place on exploring a situation in human relations so that the participants see things more clearly and can act accordingly. Shirley received further supplies of her medication plus an extra homoeopathic remedy for sluggish kidney function. She knows that she can return whenever she needs attention.

More Dimensions in Psychology

In Chapter 10 the esoteric constitution involving the subtle part of our being was discussed. This mechanism involves the astral and mental body as vehicles for our emotions and thoughts. Our inner essence or soul was mentioned in terms of the healing factor within each individual which can be invoked by the personality through both psychological work and the alignment provided by meditation.

Recently, I have been working with groups of therapy-resistant patients using discussion and a creative form of meditation to develop the daily experience of alignment with our inner soul or essence to provide a healing integrating factor in the personality. We have been meeting once weekly over a six-week period and participants receive a tape of the meditation as undertaken in the group for use at home. Although I intended the preliminary sessions mainly to feature instruction and discussion about the esoteric mechanism for our consciousness, in practice it has worked out differently. A number of psychological issues have been raised depending on the particular problems of the individuals and, where appropriate, the esoteric philosophy has been woven into these discussions if it provides a helpful framework for growth and understanding.

For instance, the issue of free choice has been continually raised. This concept has been discussed in terms of choosing health or disease and then this leads on to a deeper discussion as to the possibility of reincarnation and choices which are made (possibly before birth) as to our parents, place of birth and genetic inheritance according to karma from previous lives. The whole mechanism for reincarnation is then sometimes debated and the parallel issue of death, withdrawal from life and the varying ways people die, both psychologically and physically, emerges. I find that people find it very meaningful to discuss these issues in terms of their own experiences.

Many persons have out-of-the-body experiences but have been reticent about discussing them for fear of ridicule. Having experienced their consciousness as separate from their brain, they are naturally very interested to discuss the large body of teachings on the subject which has come to us from the East. Other discussions range around the variety of transcendental states which people experience beyond the normal physical sensations, feelings and thoughts of our personality life.

Another main issue involves the experience of group members with older family members who are gradually withdrawing from life and who appear to be undergoing some kind of personality disintegration. The senility and lack of recognition of family members and present events can be very puzzling in the light of a materialistic philosophy. In esoteric psychology, the process is accepted as the withdrawal—sometimes by many years—of the soul prior to death of the physical body. Following withdrawal, the personality in terms of the feeling nature and lower mind gradually becomes lacking in co-ordination and direction and a more vegetative and child-like existence manifests. This takes place because the soul is the integrating factor.

The aim of these group discussions could be seen as revealing to participants the various levels on which their consciousness functions, using simple common experiences involving our everyday sensations, feelings and thoughts and then to search for examples in our lives which could be classed as 'peak' experiences when our consciousness is temporarily elevated to a more meaningful and intrinsic level of being. The meditation process enables us to have control over these healing insightful states and allows us to invoke them at will. It is a gradual process and by means of meditating regularly with the group, the strength of the process is enhanced so that the individual actually begins to experience energy flows which are healing.

The meditation process which is taught is patterned on the breathing rhythm. There is first an alignment which relates to inhalation and this is designed in three stages. First, there is a relaxation of the physical body using a visualisation of light which we move around all parts of the body. We then focus on our feelings or astral nature and imagine lying in a crystal clear, calm pool of water with the sunlight streaming through the water and we see negative emotions flowing into the water where they are transmuted by the sunlight. We then focus at the mental level through visualising the mind as a many-faceted diamond which can reflect truth from all angles. Our whole personality is then understood as totally integrated and aligned.

The higher interlude is described as the pause between in-breathing and out-breathing (metaphorically speaking). We use this time, which may be extended from 3 to 8 minutes or longer, for quiet reflection on a seed thought. One method used is to build all the highest qualities imaginable into the heart centre between the shoulder blades—the heart chakra. Having exhausted all ideas we maintain a position of quiet poise and alignment to allow the spiritual energies from our higher self to permeate every part of our being. Very quiet and formless music has been found valuable to accompany the meditation work.

Exhalation or precipitation involves gathering up the energies received in meditation and doing something creative with them. Sometimes we send them around the circle and this is always experienced as a powerful flow of positive energy by nearly everyone in the group. We also individually send positive radiant energy to surround someone we know who is in need and visualise them as radiant and healthy. As the final part of our exhalation of energies we allow them to flow down to clarify our lower mind, stabilise and make serene our feeling/astral nature and recharge and energise the etheric/physical nature. The whole process is usually timed to take about 20 minutes.

In addition, we use a healing radiatory meditation taken from *Esoteric Healing* by Bailey and for this group meditation someone chooses to be the client for that session. It is a way of enabling group members to take their mind off themselves and to learn to use healing energy in a positive way. The client usually experiences the energy in a very positive and moving way and this is encouragement to group members to work in this subjective manner to heal their problems.

This approach to psychology is quite different from the orthodox approach. The aim is to lift the eyes of the personality —emotions and mind—off the problem and to create a healing focus at a more central level, and to enable the person actually to experience the energies flowing from that level. A common experience is that if the emphasis can be taken off the problem by this form of substitution, resolution of the health disorder can follow rapidly. It should be stressed that this approach may not be suitable for persons with severe personality disorders and is not advocated for persons suffering from genuine psychiatric illnesses. Very often the type of person who benefits is the typical naturopathic client who has chosen to take responsibility for their own health, but who has become therapy-resistant. This resistance may stem from a variety of common emotional conflicts, conditioning, anxieties or simply the over-active but not always productive mind which frequently accompanies the condition of starting to search for the meaning of health and life.

It has been a rewarding experience to work with people in this way and to help them find their inner essence or being and thus to move towards health. One of the first indications that this process is working is to witness the creativity which starts to manifest in the life. The soul is the creative force in our being as it is focused on the higher mental level or realm of ideas. To restore health is to create or recreate our personal environment—the physical, astral and mental vehicles so that the soul can manifest more fully in this personal environment.

On a large scale this results in health movements of various kinds—ecology, conservation, education, technological aid to under-developed countries, and sharing of planetary resources. If we consider health on a global scale, we can understand that the planetary etheric will be dramatically affected by positive initiatives of this kind.

_____CASE HISTORIES _____

Michelle had attended my clinic for an epileptic condition over a period of eighteen months. She made considerable progress with her general health with mineral combinations and vitamin B-complex for the central nervous system, herbal tablets for relaxing the nerves, specific homoeopathic remedies such as Bufo for epilepsy, and Bach flower remedies for balancing the emotions. Her general energy improved and a persistent rash under the arm was resolved with lymphatic and liver herbs in combination with the other treatment for general nervousness.

Her epileptic tendency was improved but still remained and Michelle had a constant fear and sadness hanging over her which was experienced as a heavy block near the solar plexus chakra. Meditation was discussed on several occasions and she had started to practise meditation and had undertaken a course in creative visualisation. It was of interest that a stubborn haemorrhoid tendency remained and was resistant to all therapy. This gave a clue to a deep unresolved resentment. Michelle experienced a lack of the will to live, although she was not suicidal. She also experienced uncertainty as to how to handle the negative feelings which rose up during meditation, not knowing whether to fight them or go down into them to understand their origin. To the casual outsider Michelle gave the impression of a sensitive, intelligent person with a sunny outer presence.

When I mentioned the idea of starting a meditation course for the patients, Michelle was one of the first to show interest. She felt the benefit of the meditation process which we followed and enjoyed the psychological interaction between group members. She still was unable to resolve the block in her psyche and still experienced negative emotional states during meditation. I suggested that she and I do some private sessions to allow more time for the resolution of these under-currents in her life. We meditated for about 45 minutes together each session and used the same alignment process described above.

At the first session I suggested to Michelle that she try to maintain the position of the detached observer resting in her inner being or soul when the negative feelings started to come up. My part was to maintain alignment with my soul so that healing energies could flow through to her soul whenever needed during the process. During the relaxation using light she already began to feel almost overpowered by darkness, so strong were the energies waiting to be released. She then re-experienced her death as a very sad old woman in her previous incarnation. This was followed by her rebirth into the present incarnation and the experience of the harsh lights of the delivery room plus the devastating experience of bringing the same sadness into the present incarnation.

Michelle then relived her present life in childhood days and saw how she had developed a nervous trick of blanking out from reality by developing the abilty to experience flashing lights through her head. Perhaps this habit formed the basis for her epilepsy. She also experienced herself in childhood as quite often hovering over her body. The sadness continued throughout childhood into adulthood. The next experience during the first session was that the psychic block near the solar plexus centre began to move upwards towards her throat, and she struggled to permeate this blockage with light and to prevent a feeling that she was going to suffocate. Finally, she was released and the negative blockage dissolved away. This stage was experienced as light streaming into her like streams of coloured tinsel and she felt a wonderful sensation of relief and lightness and a new direction. At this stage I also experienced her aura as greatly expanding and becoming lighter.

Michelle described how she had made an effort to maintain the position of the observer and although this had been very difficult for her I think that this was the key to the success of the session. It was significant that the haemorrhoids stopped bothering Michelle after this experience.

We did another session five days later, as although she was much improved there was still some experience of the psychic blockage. Michelle had become very conscious of a gap in the alignment between her vehicles and felt that this would probably coincide with the inabilty to maintain her alignment each day and would give the epileptic tendency. This gap was probably between the etheric and astral levels.

At the second session she felt a strong impression not to dwell on the negative block and sadness any further. I also had the impression that this session was to be on a different line and endeavoured to do the radiatory healing alignment with the aim of assisting the healing process. Michelle experienced the healing of her gap in alignment as the main benefit of this session. She again relived childhood experiences and recalled her ability to meditate at times even as a child, thus indicating the positive side of her nature even when very young.

At the next group session, Michelle reported having a most disturbing week as she felt that she was on the verge of an epileptic fit all week. She was very nervous about continuing her meditative experiences because of this feeling of dread which apparently commenced paradoxically after the experience of complete alignment following the second private session. On questioning, she did admit that the block around the solar plexus had not returned, and it was suggested that the experience of this present week was a type of healing crisis resulting from the moving around in her psyche of the previous block. She mentioned a further block in the head area which had not yet shifted.

The next evening a further private meditation session took place and it was agreed that this would not be an exploration into the past or into any of the problems but a healing session to consolidate the previous gains and to eradicate and resolve for good the lack of alignment, the gaps and the final blockage in the head area. Michelle was very aware of the healing energies which flowed through and around her during most of the session. She felt positive at the end of the session and found that the blockage in the head had gone. She mentioned the recognition of a source of power and energy from within herself. A definite turning point appeared to have been reached where although there were some times when she felt disturbances within, the basic fear and sadness had disappeared, and in their place was the experience of a central point of emerging life and love.

As Michelle had attended a number of counsellors and psychological programmes without help for her basic problem, this is a good case to illustrate the benefit of teaching people how to short-circuit their problems using soul energies. The material worked through in that first session may have taken months to unravel, if it became unravelled at all, using either traditional or modern psychological approaches. There is still further work to be done by Michelle—not all blockages have been cleared but she has experienced some positive growth.

One of the exciting aspects of working with this first group of clients was to see how they began to take a great interest in joining in the healing process of each other and the amazing potential which began to be released. The majority of the twelve had not meditated before and it must be remembered that, in the beginning, they were therapy-resistant patients. During the sixth session, I suggested that when we undertook the radiatory healing meditation I would use the magnetic healing technique to work on Brian to enhance immunity via the heart chakra. Meanwhile they would endeavour to keep their alignment of soul, mind, brain, and aura to enhance the whole process as a group.

Brian had been diagnosed with a very severe form of malignancy and was undergoing extensive chemotherapy. He had responded very well to the basic naturopathic treatment and to the chemotherapy and was meditating regularly every day. He had already outlived his prognosis by some weeks and had managed to keep up his usual work life as well. At this point, he had made the courageous decision not to continue the chemotherapy.

For the first time during meditation, he experienced colours of yellow and orange enfolding him during the healing process. One other group member who was new to meditation experienced the same colours around Brian. Orange is the colour of vitality and yellow is associated with the immune system. This consistency in observations is actually quite rare even between life-long clairvoyants.

The group was originally programmed for six weeks but they all wished to continue on a weekly basis. Their daily meditation had begun to enhance their lives and health. This combination of natural physical remedies, creative thought and meditation promises much for a new medical and totally holistic therapeutic process.

CHAPTER 13

Medicine of the Future

How will natural therapies develop in the future? Will natural therapists be recognised and able to work with orthodox medicine? What sort of training do natural therapists undertake now and will this change in the future? How can bridges be built between orthodox and complementary medicine? What are the economic implications of natural medicine?

Creativity and Natural Therapies

To practise natural therapies is to have a very creative occupation. Each client is treated as an individual and the blend of therapies used for each person is unique. The therapist gradually educates patients into new life-styles and an understanding of the causes of health and disease. This calls forth creative activity from the patients as they gradually transform their lives and observation of this creative change is very rewarding. The following paragraph from *Esoteric Healing* by Alice Bailey summarises this approach:

> Methods of healing and techniques of alleviation are peculiar to humanity and are the result of man's mental activity. They indicate his latent power as a creator, and as one who progresses

183

towards freedom. They indicate his discriminative ability to sense perfection, to vision the goal, and hence to work towards ultimate liberation.[1]

The factor of the soul or spiritual essence within the centre of our being has been discussed in Chapter 10. It is the soul which is the creative factor in any project because it is coloured by energies of the higher mental plane. An increasing number of people are now becoming conscious of their soul through meditation and reflective thought. In terms of health and well-being this means a search for creative solutions to health problems. Natural therapies are at the forefront of this creative activity.

In keeping with this trend, the clients of natural therapists are inclined to be well educated, self-aware, and tend to take responsibility for their own health. The flow-on of their creative attitudes is observed in how they tend to spread ideas and techniques about natural therapies through their families and friends. For this reason, most of our clients come by word of mouth, and not by advertising or because of any government recognition or subsidy. One positive outcome of this situation is that only those therapists with integrity, who can help produce healthy changes in the client, remain on the scene for any length of time.

More recently, a new phase has commenced and this has implications for the future of natural therapies in terms of education and government recognition. In Chapter 1, the main traditional therapies of clinical nutrition (vitamin and mineral therapy), herbal medicine, and homoeopathy were detailed. Acupuncture is also a main traditional therapy but has never enjoyed the popularity in Australia of the other main therapies. However, due to the medical interest in acupuncture it has been the first natural therapy to be introduced into the state education systems, although at the time of writing funding had not yet been approved.

The auxiliary therapies were also briefly described in Chapter 1 and these have expanded in a variety of directions since the last government enquiry into natural therapies within

Australia. This has provided a major headache for educators in the field. Various government inquiries into natural therapies have taken place in Australia over the last fifteen years. This overview will demonstrate the considerable changes which have taken place in terms of the government view and attitudes towards natural therapies.

Recognition of Natural Therapies

As one of the senior educators within the sphere of natural therapies in Australia, I have been able to observe the growth of natural therapies over the period of its greatest expansion. In 1973 I had only been involved with the education scene for just over one year when an all-party State enquiry into naturopathy took place in Victoria. At first this was intended to be an investigation into chiropractic medicine only but it was extended to include naturopathy. Members of the investigating committee involved parliamentary members with no medical or scientific training. Prejudice was voiced openly from the beginning of the enquiry and it was not surprising when the *Report Upon Osteopathy, Chiropractic and Naturopathy* was published in 1975 that there was very little support suggested for either recognition of the profession or support or subsidy of the training. One positive comment related to the founding of the Southern School of Natural Therapies by Alfred Jacka: 'Mr Jacka's efforts to establish a significant school have been remarkable and have produced abundant evidence to support his enthusiasm for the need to have adequate training'.[2]

This report had hardly been digested when a Commonwealth enquiry, with a leading academic as chairperson, was established in the same year as the tabling of the Victorian report. This committee contained more persons qualified in medicine and science than had the State enquiry, but it soon became obvious that there was bias even before investigations were completed. Several members of the committee were from the orthodox medical profession and no members had any prior understanding of natural therapies. There was no attempt to make an unbiased or systematic inquiry into either the practice or principles of natural therapies, and no adequate investigation of patients, patients' records or treatment programmes was undertaken. There was no assessment of public attitudes towards natural therapies.

The Webb report, as it was colloquially named (after the chairman, Professor Webb), was published in 1977. It recommended registration for chiropractic and osteopathy but saw no necessity or possibility for recognition of naturopathy, the term used to cover the internal therapies involving the use of minerals, vitamins, herbs and homoeopathy. In contrast, at this time public interest in naturopathy was already demonstrated by attendance at classes conducted by the Technical and Further Education division of the Education Department. I had designed and was lecturing in three ten-week series which attracted ninety pupils for each series. This interest continued for the nine years I continued to lecture for the Council for Adult Education. The class lists revealed that many professionals, in particular nurses and teachers, were amongst the participants.

During the early 1980s, as interest in and experience of natural therapies grew among members of the general public, natural therapists were plagued by a series of official moves to restrict their practice. Initiatives for these restrictions were usually traced to the same source and much time and energy was spent educating the government in the real facts.

The most significant move was the Draft Standard on Vitamins and Minerals to which natural therapists were alerted in 1981. This Draft Standard was worded in such a way that our access to the type of remedies we habitually used would have been severely restricted. After we had alerted the general public to the situation, 250 000 letters were sent by concerned individuals to Federal parliamentary members. The Draft Standard on Vitamins and Minerals disappeared from the scene.

In 1984 another attempt to restrict natural therapies came in the form of a piece of legislation entitled the Therapeutic,

Goods and Cosmetic Bill. Once again, much effort was put into alerting the public to the possibility of all natural medicines suffering complete restriction. After advice from a number of legal sources it appeared definite that if the Bill was passed all natural medicines would have to be subject to the same clinical trials as pharmaceutical drugs. In the case of herbal medicine and homoeopathy, this was an impossible task due to the very individual way of prescribing these therapies. There was also the enormous cost of the trials for the many thousands of homoeopathic remedies in their various potencies.

After considerable pressure from the public again, the Bill was withdrawn in spring and an all-parliamentary party inquiry in the form of the Victorian State Government Social Development Committee was given the task of investigating the parameters of the proposed Bill, and of inquiring into all aspects of natural therapies. For the first time, a committee decided to do an unbiased and professional investigation. The *Report of Alternative Medicine and Health Food Industry* was the most detailed and thorough of any inquiries into natural therapies throughout the world.

All interested parties were invited to make formal submissions and the hearings stretched over many weeks. Everyone who had made a submission was invited to discuss it. Extensive surveys were undertaken by trained research assistants into the training, practice and clinics involving natural therapies. A market survey was conducted amongst some thousands of members of the general public. Similar detailed investigations involved the health food industry and the retail outlets known as health food stores. Members of the government committee travelled overseas to gather further data. Naturopaths were not aware of bias or prejudice and our impression was that the committee members were genuinely interested in understanding natural therapies in all aspects.

The report was tabled in two sections. The first involved the Therapeutic Goods and Cosmetic Bill in December 1985. The second part, entitled *Inquiry into Alternative Medicine and the*

Health Food Industry, was tabled in parliament during December 1986. It is worth quoting a short section from the chairperson's preface:

> The committee is unanimous in its conclusion that alternative medicine plays a very significant role in the life of many Victorians. For example, nearly 400,000 Victorian adults have used the services of alternative medicine practitioners in the last year; approximately 1.5 million people have used vitamins over the last five years, and of those who currently use alternative remedies such as vitamins, about six out of ten say they take them at least once per week. Such figures indicate that health authorities and others must recognise their responsibilities in the regulation of this important area of primary health care.[3]

Recommendations from the first report involving therapeutic substances included the establishment of a two-tier system of registration of therapeutic goods. Natural therapies could be exempt under this system from the type of clinical trials undergone by drugs provided they did not have labelling which made claims. Quality control was seen as necessary in both tiers and was not disputed by anyone. As yet the report has not been debated in parliament.

The second report contained one major disappointment for natural therapists with a recommendation that natural therapists did not need registration. A number of other recommendations were to our satisfaction and these included suggestions as to greater co-operation between orthodox and alternative medicine, and the establishment of a uniform basic science course for all natural therapists: 'That the Ministry for Education liaise with alternative medicine associations and training institutions to establish guidelines for the development of basic health science courses'.[4]

One recommendation caused natural therapists some amusement and relief. It was observed by the committee that orthodox medical persons sometimes practised using natural therapies with very little training in the area. This had been a cause of concern to our profession for some time. The committee's recommendation indicated that the committee did not have the bias of the previous inquiries into natural medicine: 'That an expert committee appointed by the Health Department of Victoria investigate the adequacy or otherwise of training of orthodox medical practitioners in alternative diagnostic or therapeutic techniques, in conjunction with representatives of the relevant alternative medicine professions'.[5]

During the period of this latest enquiry many individuals approached our training institution for upgrading and expected that registration would be the outcome. They sought to become eligible in various ways to equip themselves for accreditation with the Australian Natural Therapists Association. After the report was tabled, poorly trained therapists realised that they need not make any efforts in this direction. There was a proliferation of fringe activities and of new training institutions staffed by people without basic science or medical training. Well-trained therapists started receiving many complaints from members of the general public who had visited a variety of self-styled and largely self-taught persons.

Since the end of the enquiry, registration of natural therapists has taken place in the Northern Territory and other State governments have asked for further information from the naturopathic associations about registration. It is only a matter of time before registration will take place. A form of recognition has taken place from private health funds. All these funds give rebates to natural therapists who are accredited with the Australian Natural Therapists Association. This recognition was established as a result of training standards.

Education and Natural Therapies

It has been suggested by leading tertiary educators from both the State Education Departments and the naturopathic profession in Australia that a suitable course of training for natural therapists must be at least 3000 hours in length and must contain a considerable proportion of basic medical sciences. These include anatomy, physiology, chemistry, biochemistry, nutrition, clinical diagnosis and pathology. High standards have also been established in the main traditional therapies of vitamins, minerals, herbal medicine and homoeopathy. As mentioned, acupuncture has already been integrated into State education departments although funding has yet to be approved. In addition, graduates must have had considerable practical training under supervision in an approved clinic. A comprehensive professional indemnity scheme is available for graduates who undergo the training prescribed by the Australian Natural Therapists Association. At the Southern School of Natural Therapies, the oldest naturopathic school in Australia, about forty graduates per year go out into the community to make their contribution towards health care in this country. Schools in the other states are rapidly developing in the same direction.

In spite of the proliferation of sub-standard courses which has taken place since the last enquiry in 1986, there is still a consistent demand for high-standard training at the approved courses. There is concern with the increasing number of poorly trained therapists who are treating the public. The main problem is more likely to be a sin of possible omission in treatment, rather than the causing of any particular harm by the wide range of fringe therapies which are used. In other words, without training in pathology and symptomatology, these fringe operators are likely to miss the need for referral for orthodox treatment. This can be dangerous in conditions like appendicitis, severe diarrhoea, pneumonia, and a number of other acute conditions.

It is only a matter of time before this situation is rectified by government. Members of the general public are now so interested in natural therapy that they are sometimes inclined to rush off to a therapist without checking the therapist's credentials. One safeguard, which is now occurring more frequently, is the increasing co-operation between individual doctors and natural therapists. It is natural that orthodox physicians will work with well-trained therapists.

Bridging the Gap between Orthodox and Complementary Medicine

One of the recommendations in the 1986 Victorian parliamentary report was to the effect that

> the Minister for Health recommends to the next Health Ministers' conference that the Commonwealth Department of Health, together with the Health Department of Victoria and other State Health Departments, establish a standards setting mechanism to develop guidelines regarding the issue of cross-referral between qualified medical practitioners and practitioners of alternative medicine and vice versa.[6]

The present policy of the Australian Medical Association discourages its members from referring patients to practitioners of alternative medicine but they are not forbidden to do so on occasions where they feel such treatment is appropriate. It should be pointed out, however, that 30 per cent of active medical practitioners do not belong to this association. There are two other medical associations in Australia.

Over the years that natural therapies have developed there has been a gradual and growing interest in them among members of the orthodox medical profession. Some individuals have studied single subjects at the Southern School of Natural Therapies, others have increasingly referred patients to natural therapists, and a few younger medical graduates have practised in clinics which are represented by a number of disciplines. In the future, the ideal situation will be a number of clinics where a variety of disciplines will be available. These can include orthodox medicine, psychology, naturopathy, acupuncture and chiropractic. A central secretarial office with an appropriately trained person could help clients decide which would be the most appropriate discipline to start with the treatment of their problem.

With more opportunity for uniform training developing in each State, there is no reason why orthodox medicine in the near future need have any fear about recommending clients to natural therapists. Another profession which is moving towards a more holistic image is dentistry, and dentists are also beginning to work more openly with natural therapists.

The following areas are examples of where there can be useful co-operation between orthodox medicine and natural therapists. In the case of elective surgery it is of advantage for the patient to have at least one month of natural medicine before and after surgery. This includes herbs for lymphatic drainage, vitamin C for detoxification and wound healing, general nerve treatment with minerals and vitamin B-complex, vitamin E to prevent thrombosis and to promote healing, and zinc to prevent haemorrhage following surgery and to promote healing. Many surgeons have been agreeably surprised by the rapid recovery of patients who are taking natural medicine before and after surgery.

Another area of great potential for co-operation is pregnancy and childbirth. Many women now take natural medicine throughout the pregnancy and during labour. For instance, when treating pregnant clients my approach is to give calcium and iron phosphate, replacing the latter with vitamin E halfway through the pregnancy. Raspberry Leaf tablets are given after the sixth month to strengthen the uterine muscle and this tends to shorten the labour period. Vitamin C is given throughout the pregnancy to inhibit any viruses, detoxify environmental pollutions and thus lessen the likelihood of birth defects. Homoeopathic Caulophyllum in the 30th potency is given during the last two months to ensure the baby takes up the right position before labour. I have had experience of clients whose babies completely turned around from breech to normal position a few days after taking this remedy. Meanwhile, the prospective mother attends the orthodox practitioner throughout her pregnancy. If there is acceptance on the part of the doctor for using natural medicine, particular homoeopathic remedies and acupuncture can be very useful during the actual labour period.

There are a number of areas of chronic disease where a joint naturopathic and orthodox approach is desirable. In many cases of circulatory disease, patients must stay on their pharmaceutical drugs, for instance in cases of very high blood pressure. At the same time they can be taking herbs, minerals such as magnesium and particular homoeopathic remedies to rebalance the biochemistry. If improvement takes place they can gradually reduce their drugs under medical supervision. A nervous condition like epilepsy is another situation where drugs may be essential to control fits and where natural medicine can be taken concurrently to improve the general health and to gradually reduce the tendency to convulsions. In my previous book I outline an outstanding case in this respect.[7]

One area where co-operation between two health professions is increasing is that between registered chiropractors and naturopaths. A number of recent graduates of chiropractic are tending to refer patients to natural therapists and vice versa. The use of particular minerals and homoeopathic remedies can enhance the structural integrity of the spine and surrounding ligaments and muscles so that less manipulation of the spine is needed.

At the moment, the situation between the natural and orthodox profession is that patients tend to take natural therapies for conditions without necessarily telling the orthodox doctor. Increasingly, there appears to be a more overt co-operation which can only benefit the patient in many ways.

Economic Factors and Natural Therapies

The professions of natural therapies envisage enormous savings to any government which actively supports, recognises and subsidises natural therapies. It has been demonstrated that persons who regularly take natural medicine have fewer days off work and this factor alone would save industry millions of dollars. Apart from actual decrease of absenteeism, the enhancement of well-being described by people taking natural therapies is a major factor in individuals feeling they are more efficient at their work tasks. This is a frequent comment by clients.

Another significant area of cost saving is in the number of surgical conditions which could be prevented using natural therapies. These include tonsillectomies, appendicectomies, varicose veins and haemorrhoids, hernias and prolapses, orthopaedic surgery such as knee cartilages and some spinal surgery, gall-bladder surgery, and uterine surgery for fibroids. Much expense could also be alleviated if natural therapies could be used for accident victims in their recuperative phase.

In the area of geriatric care, many elderly people are kept in good health throughout their autumn years by attending a natural therapist several times per year and taking simple remedies to maximise their energy and immunity. Strokes can be prevented, arthritis minimised, memory and concentration preserved, and the joy of life continued until the person dies a natural death. The cost of nursing homes is an enormous burden to any government and this cost could be substantially reduced.

Natural therapies are here to stay. The general public support and encourage a creative approach to resolving health problems and enhancing well-being and wholeness. It remains for natural healing to be fully integrated with the health care systems throughout the world and for governments to recognise how natural therapies can creatively complement orthodox medicine in many ways. It is the destiny of humanity to restore their health and to experience life more abundantly.

NOTES

CHAPTER 1
The Main Therapies and Their Blending

1 Jacka, J., *A–Z of Natural Therapies*. Lothian (Melbourne, 1987).

2 Solecki, R. S. and Shansdar, I. V., 'A Neanderthal Flower Burial in Northern Iraq', *Science* (1975) 190:880–1.

3 Thomson, W. A. R., *Healing Plants: A Modern Herbal*. McGraw Hill (London, 1978); Griggs, B. *Green Pharmacy: A History of Herbal Medicine*. Jill Norman and Hobhouse (London, 1981).

4 Banerman, R. H., *et al.*, *Traditional Medicine and Health Care Coverage*. World Health Organisation (Geneva, 1983) 9–13, 50–8, 68–75.

5 Griggs, B., op. cit.

6 Hutchins, R. M. (ed.), *Hippocratic Writings: Great Books of the Western World*. Encyclopedia Britannica (London, 1952).

7 Stuart, M. (ed.), *The Encyclopedia of Herbs and Herbalism*. Orbis (London, 1982).

8 Boericke, W., and Dewey, W., *The Twelve Tissue Salts*. Set Dey and Co. (Calcutta, 1959).

9 Blackmore, M. C. H. *Mineral Deficiencies in Human Cells*. Blackmore Laboratories (Sydney, n.d.).

10 Regtop, H., 'Is Magnesium the Grossly Neglected Mineral?' *Int. Clin. Nutr. Rev.* (1983) 3 (3) 10–20.

11 Abstract. *Int. Clin. Nutr. Rev.* (1982) 3 (4) 47: 'Beneficial Effect of Chromium Supplementation', *J. AMA* (1982) 247: 3046–7.

12 Pfieffer, C., *Zinc and Other Micro-Nutrients*. Keats (Connecticut, 1978).

13 Lesser, M., *Nutrition and Vitamin Therapy*. Grove Press (New York, 1980).

14 Jacka, J., op. cit.

15 Mount, L., *The Food and Health of Western Man*. Precision Press (Buckshire, UK, 1979) 1–21.

16 Grossinger, R., *Planet Medicine*. Anchor Books (New York, 1980).

17 Callinan, P. 'Vibratory Energy in Water: A Model for Homeopathic Action', *J. Complementary Medicine* (Feb. 1986) 2: 34–53.

18 Drury, N. (ed.), *The Body Work Book*. Harper and Row (Sydney, 1984).

CHAPTER 2
Vitality and Energy Patterns in Health and Disease

1 Grossinger, R., *Planetary Medicine: From Stone Age Shaminism to Post Industrial Healing*. Shambala Press (London, 1982).

2 *A Submission to the Social Development Committee of the Parliament of Victoria on the Status and Practice of Natural Therapies*, vol. 1. The Australian Natural Therapist Association (Melbourne, 1985).

3 Capra, F., *The Turning Point*. Bantam Books (London, 1983) ch. 10.

4 Zhu Zong-xiangi, 'Research Advances in the Electrical Specificity of Meridians and Acupuncture Points', *American J. Acupuncture* (1981) 9 (3) 203–15.

5 Boyd, W. E., 'Biochemical and Biological Evidence for the Activity of High Potencies', *Br. Homoeopathic J.* (1984) 54.

6 Jensen, B., *Iridology – The Science and Practice in the Healing Arts*. Bernard Jensen Publishing (California, 1982) 2–6.

7 Ibid. 83–5; Deck, J., *Principles of Iris Diagnosis*. Institute for Fundamental Research on Iris Diagnosis (Ettlingen, 1982).

CHAPTER 3
Medical Science and the Energy Factor

1 Burr, H. S., *Blueprint for Immortality*. Neville Spearman (London, 1972) 33.

2 Ibid., 137–53.

3 Gerard, R. W. and Liber, B., 'The Control of Normal and Convulsive Brain Potentials', *American J. Psychiatry* (1940) 96:1125.

4 Becker, R. O. and Marino, A., *Electromagnetism and Life*. State University of New York Press (Albany, 1982) 39.

5 Marsh, G. and Beams, H. W., 'Electrical Control of Morphogenesis in Regenerating Dugesic Tigrinum', *J. Cell. Comp. Physiol.* (1952) 39:191.

6 Huggins, C. and Yang, N. C., 'Induction and Extinction of Mammary Cancer', *Science* (1962) 137:257.

7 Becker, R. O. and Marino, A., op. cit.

8 Moss, T., *The Body Electric*. J. P. Tarcher (Los Angeles, 1978).

9 Johnson, K. *The Living Aura*. Hawthorn Books (New York, 1975).

10 Sheldrake, R., *A New Science of Life*. Paladin (London, 1983) 13, 14.

CHAPTER 4.
Etheric Energy, Science and Medicine

1 Reid, B. L., 'Propagation of Properties of Chemical Reactions Over Long Distance in the Atmosphere as seen by Crystal Growth Pattern Changes', *Aust. J. Med. Lab. Sci.* (1986) 7:30–35.

2 Reid, B. L., 'The Great Energy Debate: The Place of Subtle Energy', *Aust. J. Homoeopathy*, (April 1987) 1.

3 Reid, B. L., 'Biological Action at a Distance: A Contribution from Biology to Investigations of the Paranormal', in Zollschan, G. K. (ed.), *et. al.*, *Exploring the Paranormal*. Prism (Bridport, Dorset, in press).

4 Husemann, F. and Wolff, O., *The Anthroposophical Approach to Medicine*. Vol. I (New York, 1982) 163–81.

5 Prechter, R. J. and Frost, A. J. *The Elliot Wave Principle*. New Classic Library (New York, 1978).

6 Reid, B. L., 'The Great Energy Debate: The Place of Subtle Energy', *Aust. J. Homoeopathy*, (April 1987) 1.

CHAPTER 5
Using Bio-energetic Medicine

1 Voll, R., 'Twenty Years of Electro Diagnosis in Germany: A Progress Report', *American J. Acupuncture* (1975) 3: 7–17.

2 Kenyon, J., *Modern Techniques of Acupuncture*, vol. 3. Thorsons (London, 1985).

3 Becker, O. and Marino, A. *Electromagnetism and Life*. State University of New York Press (Albany, 1982) 70–5.

4 Kenyon, J., op. cit.

5 Tiberiu, R. and Gheorge, G., 'Do Meridians of Acupuncture Exist: A Radioactive Tracer Study of the Bladder Meridian', *American J. Acupuncture* (July–Sept. 1981) 9 (3) 251–5; Tiller, W., 'What Do Electrodermal Diagnostic Acupuncture Instruments Really Measure?' *American J. Acupuncture* (Jan.–March) 15 (1) 15–23.

6 Russell, E. W., *Report on Radionics*. Neville Spearman (London, 1973).

CHAPTER 6
Practical Applications of Bio-energetic Medicine

1 Kenyon, J., *21st Century Medicine*. Thorsons (London, 1986).

2 Fehrenbach, J., *et al. Short Manual of the Vegatest Method*. Vega (Schiltach, W. Germany, 1986).

3 Nixon, F., *Search for Vivaxis*, parts 1 & 2. Magnetic Publishers (Chemainus, Canada, 1982).

4 Pope, I., 'Austrian Research Highlights Earth Radiation as Cause of Cancer', *J. Alternative Medicine* (April 1986) 4 (4) 5–6.

5 Moore, A., 'Are You Under Geopathic Stress?', *Wellbeing* 15:94–8.

CHAPTER 7
Toxaemia — the Twentieth-Century Plague

1 Mount, J. L., *The Food and Health of Western Man*. Precision Press (Buckshire, UK, 1978) 1–21.

2 Buist, R., *Food Intolerance*. Harper and Row (Sydney, 1984).

3 Illich, I., *Limits to Medicine*. Lothian (London, 1976).

4 Tee, D., 'Another Look at the Interaction of Psyche and Soma', *Complementary Med. Res.* (Feb. 1987) 2 (1) 1–2.

5 Kriege, T., *Fundamental Basis of Iris Diagnosis*. L. N. Fowler (Essex, UK, 1977).

CHAPTER 8
The Stages of Disease

1 Coulter, H. and Fisher, B., 'Vaccination: The Pertussis Coverup is Exposed', *J. Alternative Medicine* (1985) 3 (11) 4–6.

2 Hetzel, B., *Health and the Australian Society*. Penguin (Ringwood, Vic., 1974).

3 Jacka, J., *A Philosophy of Healing*. Inkata Press (Melbourne, 1979).

CHAPTER 9
Toxaemia, Inflammation, Bacteria and Science

1 Reckeweg, H., *Homotoxicology*. Menaca Pub. Co. (New Mexico, 1984) 59.

2 Ibid., 122.

3 Hume, E. D., *Bechamp or Pasteur*. Lee Foundation for Nutritional Research (Wisconsin, 1923).

4 Bechamp, A., *The Blood and Its Third Anatomical Element*. John Ouseley (London, 1912) out of print, 337, 342.

5 Reich, W., *The Cancer Biopathy*. Farrar, Strauss and Giroux (New York, 1923).

6 Bott, V., *Anthroposophical Medicine,* Rudolf Steiner Press (London, 1978) ch. 6.

CHAPTER 10
The Subjective Factors in Toxaemia and Devitalisation

1 Blavatsky, H. B., *The Secret Doctrine*. Theosophical Publishing House (London, 1950).

2 Bailey, A. A., *Esoteric Healing*. Lucis Press (London, 1953).

3 Wilbur, K. (ed.), *The Holographic Paradigm and Other Paradoxes*. Shambahla (London, 1982) ch. 2.

4 Karagulla, S., *Breakthrough to Creativity*. De Vorss and Co. Inc. (California, 1967); Tansley, D., *Chakras, Rays and Radionics*. C. W. Daniel and Co. (Essex, UK, 1984); Lansdowne, Z., *The Chakras and Esoteric Healing*. Samuel Weiser (Maine, 1986).

5 Ferguson, M., *The Aquarian Conspiracy*. J. P. Tarcher (Los Angeles, 1987).

CHAPTER 11
The Inherited Factors in Health and Disease

1 Hahnemann, S., *The Chronic Diseases*. Ringer and Co. (India, n.d.) 29.

2 Ibid., 39.

3 Husemann, F. and Wolff, O., *The Anthroposophical Approach to Medicine*, vol. 1. Anthroposophical Press (New York, 1982) 299.

4 Bailey, A. A., *Esoteric Healing*. Lucis Press (London, 1953) 59.

5 Bailey, A. A., *Esoteric Psychology*, vol. 2. Lucis Press (London, 1942).

6 Bailey, A. A., *Esoteric Healing*. op. cit., 492.

7 Dhawale, M. L., *Principles and Practice of Homoeopathy*. Karnatak Publishing House (Bombay, 1967).

CHAPTER 12
Psychology and Natural Therapies

1 Boericke, W. and Dewey, W., *The Twelve Tissue Remedies of Schussler*, 6th edn. B. Jain (New Delhi, 1978) 74, 78.

2 Lesser, M., *Nutrition and Vitamin Therapy*. Grove Press (New York, 1980).

3 Chancellor, P. M., *Handbook of the Bach Flower Remedies*. C. W. Daniel and Co. (London, 1971).

CHAPTER 13
Medicine of the Future

1 Bailey, A. A., *Esoteric Healing*. Lucis Press (London, 1953) 13.

2 *Report Upon Osteopathy, Chiropractic and Naturopathy*. Victorian Parliament (1975) 27.

3 *Inquiry into Alternative Medicine and the Health Food Industry*. Victorian Parliament (December, 1986) xv.

4 Ibid., (v).

5 Ibid., (xii).

6 Ibid., (x).

7 Jacka, J., *A–Z of Natural Therapies*. Lothian (Melbourne, 1987) 152.

Index

remedies, 167–74
pupil of the eye, 35

radiation effects, 75–9
radiesthesia sense, 77
radionics, 67–9
reaction phase of disease, 104–5
Reckeweg, Hans-Heinrich, 103–6
Recommended Daily Allowance (RDA) of
    vitamins, 13
reductionism, 29
reflexology, 25
Reich, W., 111–14
Reid, Bevan, 19, 53–60, 116
Reiki healing, 26, 27
reincarnation,
  and inherited disease, 157–60
  mechanisms of, 159–60
  psychological aspects, 179
relaxation, 176
remedies,
  availability of natural, 186–7
  combined action of, see synergistic
      effects
  ingestion ease, 20–1
  potency, 19
  preparation, 19, 20
  testing, 187
repertories, 18
*Report of Alternative Medicine and Health
    Food Industry*, 187–8
*Report Upon Osteopathy, Chiropractic
    and Naturopathy*, 185
resonance, homoeopathic theory of, 20
retracing phenomenon, 99–100

sacral centre (chakra), 127–9
salycilates, 97
Schimmel, Helmut, 62–3
Schusslers' mineral therapy, 9
sclerosing principle, 115
Segmental Electrograph, 65
selenium, 12
sensitivity, allergic, see hypersensitivity
sensory pole, 115
sexual problems, 128–9
Sheldrake, Rupert, 50–2
similars, law of, see law of similars
skin eruptions, 146
skin resistance, diagnosis from, 62
Social Development Committee, 187
solar plexus (chakra), 129–33

soul energies, 177, 179–81
Southern School of Natural Therapies,
    185, 190, 191
spiral, logarithmic, 58–9
spiritual healing, 26–7
steroids, 97
stimuli, effects of external, 53–5
stress, remedies for, 167
sub-acute stage of disease, 92, 97–8
subjective factors of diagnosis, 63–5
sugar metabolism, 11
surgery and natural medicine, 192
sycotic miasm, 149–53
synergistic effects, 3, 12, 14–17, 21–4
synthesis of detoxification, see synergistic
    effects
synthesis of therapies, see natural
    therapies, combination for treatment
syphilitic miasm, 156–7

'T Bacilli', 111–14
Tai Chi, 25
taints, see miasms
Theophrastus of Eresus, 5
Therapeutic Goods and Cosmetic Bill,
    186–7
therapies, auxiliary, 24–8
  see also natural therapies
therapy-resistant patients, 165–6, 174–5,
    177–8
Theratest, 65
throat centre (chakra), 136–9
thrush, 83
thymus gland, 135
thyroid gland, 137
tissue salt therapy, 9
Touch For Health, 25
toxaemia, 80–90
  disease crisis and, 100–1
  organs affected, 87–8
  elimination of toxins, 2, 6–7, 87–8
  Reckeweg's theories, 104–5
transmigration, 157
triangle of energy, 101
Triangles of Health, 31
tubercular miasm, 153–5

universe, planes of the, 122–3

Vega, 65
Vegatesting, 62–4, 66–9
  biological age and, 71–4